Mathematics Assessment

A PRACTICAL

Handbook

FOR GRADES 3–5

CLASSROOM ASSESSMENT
FOR SCHOOL MATHEMATICS

Edited by

Jean Kerr Stenmark

William S. Bush

Grades 3–5 Writing Team

Charles Allen

Shelley K. Ferguson

Jennifer Gadd

Laura Coffin Koch

Drew Kravin

Diana Lambdin

Mark Rasmussen

Mathematics Assessment

A PRACTICAL

Handbook

FOR GRADES 3–5

NATIONAL COUNCIL
OF TEACHERS OF
MATHEMATICS
RESTON, VIRGINIA

Copyright © 2001 by

THE NATIONAL COUNCIL OF TEACHERS OF MATHEMATICS, INC.

1906 Association Drive, Reston, VA 20191-9988

(703) 620-9840; (800) 235-7566; www.nctm.org

Library of Congress Cataloging-in-Publication Data

Mathematics assessment : a practical handbook for grades 3–5 / edited by Jean Kerr
Stenmark, William S. Bush ; grades 3–5 writing team, Charles Allen ... [et al.].
    p. cm. — (Classroom assessment for school mathematics K–12)
  Includes bibliographical references and index.
  ISBN 0-87353-498-0
  1. Mathematics—Study and teaching (Elementary)—United States—Evaluation. I.
Stenmark, Jean Kerr. II. Bush, William S. III. Allen, Charles. IV. Classroom assessment
for school mathematics K–12.

QA135.5 .M36772 2001
372.7—dc21

2001030628

Printed in the United States of America

Table of Contents

ACKNOWLEDGMENTS

We wish to thank the educators listed below for their suggestions, examples, and student work. We applaud their willingness to explore new ways to assess their students and, more so, their willingness to share their ideas with us.

Donna Goldstein and her students

Bob Whitlow and the teachers and students of Aurora School

Kathy Regan and the students of Providence Montessori School

THE ASSESSMENT ADDENDA TASK FORCE

William S. Bush, *Chair*

Charles Allen

Florence Glanfield

Anja S. Greer

Steve Leinwand

Jean Kerr Stenmark

Dear Reader,

The National Council of Teachers of Mathematics asked our task force to create an Addenda Series to support the Assessment Standards for School Mathematics. *This book, one of six in the series, focuses on classroom assessment in grades 3–5. Three other Practical Handbooks for teachers of grades K–2, 6–8, and 9–12 also contain examples and ideas from teachers. Two Assessment Cases books present descriptions of real classrooms, students, and teachers in assessment situations. They include reflective questions to encourage discussion about important issues in assessment.*

The Assessment Standards *book tells us that classroom assessment should—*

- *provide a rich variety of mathematical topics and problem situations;*

- *give students opportunities to investigate problems in many ways;*

- *question and listen to students;*

- *look for evidence of learning from many sources;*

- *expect students to use concepts and procedures effectively in solving problems.*

Our collection of examples, reflections, explanations, and "Tips from Teachers" will help all of us explore this role of assessment in reshaping mathematics teaching and learning. We know that assessment, from observations to standardized tests, has always affected what we do in the classroom, and we looked for ways to make that a positive influence. We are trying to clarify what we want children to learn and to find better ways to see their learning.

We value the role of students in the assessment process—from setting goals to designing and using rubrics to sharing results with others. Students have specific rights in assessment. We have adapted a list of students' rights developed by Grant Wiggins, and we have included them on the next page. Please read them and think about how they affect classroom assessment.

Many people contributed to this effort. We focused on classroom assessments and had advice and help from many teachers. We tried to include examples of assessment that accurately reflect what teachers believe is important and what students are learning. These examples are the most important part of the books.

This book, A Practical Handbook for Grades 3–5, *includes advice about getting started with assessment; selecting, developing, and managing assessment tools; and using the results. Also included are samples of good assessment tasks, scoring rubrics, checklists, and observation forms. All of these may be copied for classroom use. The bibliography will help you find additional sources for tasks and more literature about current assessment practices.*

The book will not, however, give us a formula for perfect assessment. There is no "one size fits all." Although we give examples and show some teachers' thinking about their students' work, they are only partial ideas. We can use them best as starting points for local discussions. The most helpful suggestion of all is to sit down and talk with other teachers (and students and parents) about what makes sense in helping students progress.

Every student has a right to—

- do interesting work that is useful, challenging, intriguing, or provocative;

- work collaboratively with the teacher to make learning meaningful;

- know the well-defined and clearly stated criteria for assessment or grading;

- be judged according to established criteria rather than according to her or his rank among competitors;

- get genuine and frequent feedback, both for right now and for long-term progress toward the exit level;

- take part in grading or scoring that will give chances to improve performance, with assessment being recursive and continual;

- have plenty of opportunity to do work of which he or she can be proud, with revisions, self-assessment, and self-correction;

- be able to show, often and in many ways, how well she or he is doing, especially to demonstrate strengths;

- have available during assessment whatever resources were available during learning (calculators, rulers, reference books, physical models, etc.).

Mathematics Assessment: A Practical Handbook for Grades 3–5

Introduction

This is a book about assessment in the intermediate mathematics classroom. We hope that the information contained in this book will provide you with practical tools and provocative suggestions for classroom assessment. When we use the word "assessment," we refer to attempts to answer the following questions:

- How can I communicate my expectations about my students' mathematical understanding and the quality of their work?

- What do I think my students understand at this point in time? What do they think they understand?

- Does the question, task, or activity that I choose raise the mathematical issues I hope it will raise for my students? Does it provide an opportunity for them to show me what they know?

- What question, task, or activity should I pose next?

- How can I communicate to my students and others what I think they understand?

We see classroom assessment as the centerpiece of the work teachers do. We know that teachers assess their students continually, both informally (by listening, observing, and interacting with students in class) and formally (through homework, quizzes, tests, and projects).

The ideas in this book come from our own classroom experience and from the experience of colleagues from around the country. We have been guided in our work, and in writing this book, by the vision of mathematics curriculum and instruction framed in a series of influential documents, *Curriculum and Evaluation Standards for School Mathematics* (National Council of Teachers of Mathematics [NCTM] 1989), *Professional Standards for Teaching Mathematics* (NCTM 1991), *Measuring What Counts; A Conceptual Guide for Mathematics Assessment* (Mathematical Sciences Education Board [MSEB] 1993), and in particular by these standards taken from *Assessment Standards for School Mathematics* (NCTM 1995):

Standard 1: Assessment should enhance mathematics learning.

Standard 2: Assessment should promote equity.

Standard 3: Assessment should be an open process.

Standard 4: Assessment should promote valid inferences about mathematics learning.

Standard 5: Assessment should be a coherent process.

We have organized our presentation into four chapters. In the first, we set the stage by making the case for considering new ways to assess students.

The second chapter focuses on assessment tasks; specifically how to find, modify, and create them. In the third chapter, we offer ways to plan and conduct a coherent classroom assessment program. We conclude this part of the book with a discussion of scoring, grading, reporting, and using the assessment data we collect.

Each chapter contains these features:

- **Teacher-to-Teacher** and **Student-to-Teacher** letters

- Definitions of common terms (e.g., open-ended task, analytic rubric)

- **Tips from Teachers**

- Examples of tasks, student work, rubrics, and strategies for scoring and grading

- Responses to frequently-asked questions

- References to primary sources

- References to the accompanying case books

We believe that all students are capable of developing mathematical power. We also believe that how we assess students affects this development in fundamental ways. We hope this handbook, and its companion case book, provide you with the practical suggestions that you need. We also hope they provoke you to think about assessment in new ways, and that they stimulate discussion among you, your students, and your colleagues about this crucial aspect of the work of teachers.

—The 3–5 Writing Team

Getting Ready to Shift Assessment Practices: How Do I Get Started?

Teacher-to-Teacher

I've been reading about the changes in mathematics education. I've read the NCTM Curriculum and Evaluation Standards *and tried to apply them in my classroom. It's a little hard, and sometimes feels lonely, without having someone to talk to.*

Now I have a copy of the NCTM Assessment Standards. I'm really interested in what's happening with assessment because for as long as I've been teaching, the tests given in our district have had a tremendous impact on what's taugh—sometimes not for the better. I do think that we could do a better job of looking at what students learn and do in mathematics.

I'm ready to try new ideas. What I need most to help me is more information about new assessment techniques, new ways of keeping records (where in the world shall we keep all those portfolios?), new ways of looking at students' work, and some ideas about how to get support from other teachers, administrators, parents, and the community.

I love the emphasis on problem solving but still believe we need to have the basic facts and basic skills. I also know that no one resource will give me all the answers I need—experience is the way to learn.

I'm ready to try!

Changing Assessment Practices

WHY CHANGE?

We all want our students to be "mathematically powerful," but what does that mean for assessment? Developing mathematical power involves more than simply giving students harder problems. It means asking them to focus on understanding and explaining what they are doing, digging deeper for reasons, and developing the ability to know whether they can do a better job of working on a task. For instance, part of mathematical power is knowing what it takes to succeed. Giving students information about *what* will be assessed and the *criteria* to be used in judging work is necessary to helping them do better work. We may feel comfortable and secure giving traditional tests and percent-correct grades—who can argue with the solid data of percents?—but do they help students learn and help us understand what students know and can do?

From which of these tasks in **figures 1.1** and **1.2**, for example, will we get more information about what students know?

FIG. 1.1

Which of these two fractions is larger: 2/3 or 3/2?

FIG. 1.2

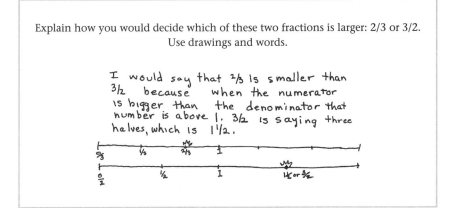

Explain how you would decide which of these two fractions is larger: 2/3 or 3/2. Use drawings and words.

I would say that 2/3 is smaller than 3/2 because when the numerator is bigger than the denominator that number is above 1. 3/2 is saying three halves, which is 1 1/2.

The NCTM *Assessment Standards for School Mathematics* (1995, p. 83) describes a set of shifts necessary to change assessment practices. Read the lists in **figure 1.3** and think about what classroom assessment might look like if the shifts are made.

FIG. 1.3

MAJOR SHIFTS IN ASSESSMENT PRACTICE (from National Council of Teachers of Mathematics [NCTM] 1995, p. 83)

TOWARD	AWAY FROM
■ Assessing students' full mathematical power	■ Assessing only students' knowledge of specific facts and isolated skills
■ Comparing students' performance with established criteria	■ Comparing students' performance with that of other students
■ Giving support to teachers and credence to their informed judgment	■ Designing "teacher-proof" assessment systems
■ Making the assessment process public, participatory, and dynamic	■ Making the assessment process secret, exclusive, and fixed
■ Giving students multiple opportunities to demonstrate their full mathematical power	■ Restricting students to a single way of demonstrating their mathematical knowledge
■ Developing a shared vision of what to assess and how to do it	■ Developing assessment by oneself
■ Using assessment results to ensure that all students have the opportunity to achieve their potential	■ Using assessment to filter and select students out of the opportunities to learn mathematics
■ Aligning assessment with curriculum and instruction	■ Treating assessment as independent of curriculum or instruction
■ Basing inferences on multiple sources of evidence	■ Basing inferences on restricted or single sources of evidence
■ Viewing students as active participants in the assessment process	■ Viewing students as the objects of assessment
■ Regarding assessment as continual and recursive	■ Regarding assessment as sporadic and conclusive
■ Holding all concerned with mathematics learning accountable for assessment results	■ Holding only a few accountable for assessment results

Changing Assessment Practices

WHAT KIND OF WORK DO WE WANT?

Below and to the right are two examples of the kind of work we might expect from students. These responses, although not perfect, are well communicated and thoughtful. They represent work that most students can do. In each instance, we might pursue further thinking by the children.

Julia is in third grade. She was given the task "You have ten cookies and there are four children. Explain how you would divide the cookies." **Figure 1.4** shows Julia's response. It is important that students be asked to respond in different ways. It is also important that we as teachers respond in ways that extend students' thinking. For instance, we might stretch Julia's thinking a bit by asking her, "What if each of the cookies was a different flavor?" or "What if you had eleven cookies?"

FIG. 1.4

Julia

First I drew four children.
Next I took ten wooden beads to act as cookies. I started by giving each child one cookie. Then I gave each kid one more cookie. I had two left over and it wouldn't be fair not to give each child the same amount. So I decided that if I cut each cookie in half and devided the halves amonge the children everyone would have the same amount of sweets,

2 ½ cookies.

CHAPTER 1

Changing Assessment Practices

Let's look at another cookie problem. Anne is in fifth grade. Her work, shown in **figure 1.5**, indicates that she may need more challenging questions than the one in this task. We might ask her whether other qualities of cookies could affect the answer (thinking of weight, thickness, density, or food value). We might get her interested in investigating number patterns that emerge if we divide different numbers of cookies among different numbers of children.

Such follow-up questions and students' responses to them tell us far more than the limited answers that we might have accepted in the past, such as "2 1/2 cookies" or "Only one can be right." Instead of looking at whether students have reached the "end of the road" by finding an answer, we want to look at how far they have come in their thinking and what we can do to help them go further.

Chapter 4 includes more examples of the kind of work that we might expect from students. Some of these examples of work are accompanied by teachers' comments.

FIG. 1.5

Paul ate 1/2 of a cookie.

Verain ate 1/2 of another cookie.

Paul said he ate more than Verain did, but Verain said he ate more than Paul did.

Could they both be right, or could only one be right?

Use drawings, words, and numbers to explain your answer.

> They couldn't both be right, because two people can't both eat more cookie than the other; it isn't possible. The possibilities are either Paul or Verain ate more than the other person, or they both ate the same amount. If the cookies were the same size and they each ate ½ they would eat the same amount, but one cookie might be bigger than the other.
>
> small cookie   BIG cookie
>
> ½ of small cookie is about ½ of ½ of big cookie

Changing Assessment Practices

WHAT KINDS OF QUESTIONS AND TASKS SHOULD WE USE?

Figures 1.6 through 1.10 show examples of assessment tasks for different purposes:

- Figure 1.6 provides a few examples of the kinds of tasks or questions that we might think about. They begin with simple and sensible tasks.

FIG. 1.6

Here's what I want to know:	Here's how I might find out:
Can the students just do the basic facts?	Determine if they respond automatically to a basic fact such as 6×7 without having to stop and think.
Do the students understand what they are doing?	Determine if they can explain how they are doing a problem.
Do the students have a strategy to go back if they forget something?	Determine if they know that $3 \times 7 = 21$, so 6×7 is the same as 3×7 plus 3×7, or $21 + 21$, or 42.
Are the students learning the new skills introduced?	Spend the last five minutes of class having students write in a journal about what they have done in class. Read some of the journals each day.
Do the students give correct or reasonable answers for simple problems?	Give them the following tasks:

- Please skip-count by 7s to 84. Use words, numbers, and pictures to explain what you know about counting by 7s.

- Does $4 \times 13 = 52$? Use words, numbers, and pictures to explain your answer.

- The product is 24. Show all the multiplication facts with 24 as the product. Tell how you worked on this task.

Assessment questions:
- Were the answers correct?
- Did the diagrams or pictures depict or show the elements of the problem?
- Were students able to explain how they arrived at their answers or whether their answers made sense?

CHAPTER *1*

Changing Assessment Practices

■ **Figure** 1.7 lists questions that might be asked to determine if students understand the concept of division.

FIG. 1.7

UNDERSTANDING THE CONCEPT OF DIVISION

Do the students understand what division means?

Can the students interpret different representations of division?

For example:

- ■ **Partitioning, or sharing—If there are 6 cookies and 2 people, how many will each person get?**

- ■ **Measuring, or repeated subtraction—If you have 6 cookies and want each person to get 3 cookies, how many people will get cookies?**

Take 35 blocks. Use the blocks to show how to do this problem: $35 \div 7 =$

Solve these two problems and explain how they are alike or different:

- ■ If you divide 35 blocks into 7 groups, how many will be in each group?

- ■ If you put 35 blocks into groups of 7, how many groups will there be?

Solve these two problems and explain how they are alike or different:

- ■ José had 6 children at his party. How would he divide 25 cookies among them?

- ■ Jamie wanted each child in the game to have 6 marbles. She had 25 marbles. How many children could be in the game?

Assessment questions:
- ■ Did students distinguish between the two forms of division?
- ■ Were their block arrangements or explanations accurate and explanatory?
- ■ Do they understand how division by grouping and by distributing are alike and different?

Changing Assessment Practices

■ **Figure 1.8** describes a task that might be used to determine if students understand geometry concepts.

FIG. 1.8

UNDERSTANDING CONCEPTS IN GEOMETRY

Do the students understand what a square is?

Please write in your journal all you know about squares.

Do the students have a basic understanding of geometric ideas and vocabulary?

Make a shapes dictionary.

Cut 10 straws into the following lengths:

■ Two straw pieces of length 3 inches

■ Two straw pieces of length 4 inches

■ Four straw pieces of length 5 inches

■ Four straw pieces of length 6 inches

Using different numbers of straw pieces, make as many polygons as you can. Use your math dictionaries to look up the names and descriptions of your shapes. Record the names and put the description in your own words.

Assessment questions:
■ Do the students understand that a square has four equal sides and four right angles? Can they draw a square?
■ Can the students identify various polygons? How well do they describe the shapes? Do they refer to the length of the sides and the number of sides and angles and so on?

Changing Assessment Practices

■ **Figure 1.9** describes tasks that might be used to assess students' understanding and applications of fractions.

FIG. 1.9

UNDERSTANDING THE CONCEPT OF FRACTIONS

Can the students show that a fraction represents equal parts of a whole and that the parts do not have to be congruent?

Here are three small grids. Find three different ways to divide the grids into fourths. Do not divide any of the cells. Color the grids with crayons to show the fractions.

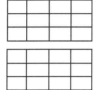

Assessment questions:

■ Are the divisions into fourths accurate, with three cells for each fourth?

■ Are the arrangements different?

■ Did the students understand that the cells used to show one-fourth could be arranged in any manner on the grid, as long as they are identified?

Can they connect the meaning of numeratior and denominator to a model or diagram?

Compare 2/3 and 3/2 Which is larger? Use blocks or a drawing to help explain your response.

Jim says that 1/4 is larger than 1/2 because 4 is larger than 2. Is he right? Explain your reasoning and the mathematics you used to find your answer.

Eddie was trying to explain the idea of the numerator and the denominator of a fraction to his brother, so he drew a diagram. Draw a diagram that he might have used, label the parts, and explain what you mean.

Assessment questions:

■ Do the students accurately use blocks or diagrams to illustrate numerator and denominator?

■ Are the explanations clear and complete?

■ Do the explanations show an understanding of the concept? Are they mathematically accurate?

Changing Assessment Practices

FIG. 1.9 (continued)

UNDERSTANDING THE CONCEPT OF FRACTIONS

Can the students show that the size of the fractional part depends on the size of the "whole"?

Your friend states that the fractions 2/3 and 5/6 are the same size because both have one "piece" fewer than the whole unit. Is your friend correct? Use words, numbers, and pictures to explain your answer.

What is the same about the two fractional parts and what is different? What fraction is shaded in each of the shapes below?

Assessment questions:

▢ Can the students explain the relationship of the various fractional parts to the whole unit?

▢ Can they distinguish between shapes that are identical in size and shape but that represent different parts of the whole?

Can they show an understanding of the relative value of a variety of fractions?

On the number line below, put these fractions in order from the smallest to the largest: 1/4, 2/3, 3/6, 1/5, 3/4.

0   1
             whole

Explain how you decided where to put each fraction.

Assessment questions:

▢ Are the fractions placed fairly close to where they should be?

▢ Do the explanations make sense?

▢ What suggestions would you make to improve or modify the responses?

CHAPTER *1*

Changing Assessment Practices

▨ **Figure 1.10** describes tasks that might assess students' ability to solve problems or apply mathematical concepts to situations outside the classroom.

FIG. 1.10

ASSESSING STUDENTS' ABILITY TO APPLY AND SOLVE PROBLEMS

Do the students have a variety of strategies to solve problems?

The October 1997 issue of *Teaching Children Mathematics* includes the article "Investigating Probability and Patterns with *The Thirteen Days of Halloween*," by Maryann Wickett. The unit begins with reading from Carol Greene's book *The Thirteen Days of Halloween* (Greene 1983).

Use that book if available, or the old "Twelve Days of Christmas," or make up a similar story about any holiday. Have the children work in groups to find a way to record how many gifts were given. In oral reports of their work, have the groups compare their strategies. (There is, of course, much more in the article—find it and try it with your class!)

Assessment questions:
▨ Were the students able to complete the mathematics for this activity?

▨ Did the students use a variety of strategies, or at least more than one?

▨ What action could we take if all the groups used the same strategy?

Do they apply the skills they have learned to problems close to real life? (This is a simplified version of a longer task or unit.)

Work with your group to make a list of the kinds of supplies we have used in class this year, such as pencils, worksheets, ruled paper, crayons, colored paper, and so on. When you have completed your list, make an estimate of how many or how much of each item we have used.

Changing Assessment Practices

FIG. 1.10 (continued)

ASSESSING STUDENTS' ABILITY TO APPLY AND SOLVE PROBLEMS

Do they apply the skills they have learned to solve problems close to real life? (This is a simplified version of a longer task or unit.)

(*Make a number line that goes from 10 to 10 000. Give each group a set of dots of different colors.*) Let's start with pencils. Use the red dots to show pencils. Put your red dot on the number line to show the number of pencils your group thinks we have used this year.

(*Have all the groups put their red dots in place.*) It looks like we had some different ideas. Would any group like to tell us their reasoning for where they put the red dot? (*Have each group explain the placement of their red dot, then see whether the groups can agree on an average, or mean.*)

Now let's do the same for paper, with green dots.

Will the same number line work?

Assessment questions:

- Did the students make reasonable estimates?
- When the first group of students put their dots on the number line, did they come reasonably close to the place that was appropriate for their estimates? What discussion topics would you suggest for the class at this point?
- Were the explanations for the placement of the dots reasonable?
- What suggestions could we make to help students revise their estimates?
- Did the estimates and dot placement improve for the second set of estimates?
- Were the results reasonable and practical?

Changing Assessment Practices

FIG. 1.10 (continued)

ASSESSING STUDENTS' ABILITY TO APPLY AND SOLVE PROBLEMS

Can the students work through complex problems that may have more than one good response?

(These investigations will need planning and student-teacher conversations. The students should be allowed and expected to develop a procedure, explain their work, show visual displays, make appropriate estimations, etc.)

How much should it cost a family to buy breakfast cereal for a week?

How can we find out how tall our school building is?

How many students would you estimate there are in our school?

Which of our textbooks has the most pages in it? The most words?

How large is our school playground?

What are the sizes of different kinds of dogs? Report your findings in at least three ways, including a display that clearly shows the differences.

How far and how fast can a fish swim? (This might be a good problem for a trip to an aquarium.)

Assessment questions:

- What evidence do we see of the accurate and appropriate use of mathematics?
- Did the students predict or estimate what their results would be?
- Did they make a plan or develop a procedure?
- Was the research or survey done in an organized way?
- Was the information organized for presentation?
- Did visual displays clearly show the information?
- Were explanations complete?
- Were groups able to explain their results or ideas to classmates?
- What questions could we ask the groups to redirect or elicit more information?

Chapter 2 includes more details about where to find assessment tasks and questions as well as other kinds of assessment.

Defining and Using Standards in Assessment

TIPS FROM TEACHERS

■ *Meet regularly with other teachers to discuss goals.*

■ *Plan assessments while planning instruction. Ask yourself, "How will I know if they have learned this?"*

■ *Gather good assessment tasks, and sort them according to units or goals.*

■ *Keep assessment in mind as you teach. Make it ongoing, part of the daily routine.*

■ *Change assessment as needed.*

■ *Look at videotapes of teachers in action.*

■ *Read about teachers who have made changes.*

WHAT ARE STANDARDS?

Standards are an effective and useful way to plan instruction and assessment. Assessment standards can be the means to tie our ideas together into a system that includes various kinds of assessment that get at different information. Standards can be defined and described in many ways. According to Glenda Lappan (1998), past president of NCTM,

> Some define "standards" as statements about the mathematics to be learned that also give levels of performance expected at each grade. Others think "standards" should specify very fine-grained behavioral objectives in mathematics for each grade. "Standards" hold many other shades of meaning that focus solely on the mathematics to be learned.

In any event, we define an **assessment standard** as a learning target or goal that defines what it means to know or be able to do something. The standard tells us where we want to go with instruction and can tell us whether we have arrived. Determining if a standard has been met requires multiple sources of evidence, such as tests, samples of students' work, written and oral responses, and ongoing classroom assessment by the teacher.

HOW CAN STANDARDS HELP US?

Assessment standards serve as a communication path linking assessment to instruction. We can let students know what their work will involve. We have a way to tell parents what to expect. Students can tell us what they know and can do. We can identify the next steps for students and for our teaching. Standards help us identify the important components of what we teach. They define the quality of students' work in general terms.

Consider, for example, the Number and Operations Standard in NCTM's (2000, p. 32) *Principles and Standards for School Mathematics*:

Instructional programs from prekindergarten through grade 12 should enable all students to—

■ understand numbers, ways of representing numbers, relationships among numbers, and number systems;

■ understand the meanings of operations and how they relate to one another;

■ compute fluently and make reasonable estimates.

It is important to develop assessments that align with our class curriculum standards, whether they are local, state or provincial, or NCTM standards. On the next page is a description of a teacher's experience with using standards in a classroom.

CHAPTER *1*

Defining and Using Standards in Assessment

One Teacher's Story about Standards

Standards for my students should reflect the current "best new idea" to improve students' learning and understanding of mathematics. After reading several articles about the role of standards and their implications for instruction, curriculum, and assessment, I decided to experiment with embedding content standards in my classroom practice.

Establishing the content and performance standards for the unit was the first step in this process. Reviewing several fractions units helped define the essential mathematics concepts for students and instruction. Two standards served as the foundation for the others. These content standards guided the instructional focus:

- A fraction represents equal parts of the whole. These parts are not necessarily congruent.

- The size of the fractional part can change depending on the size of the whole.

The content standards along with the underlying assumptions facilitated the development of instructional decisions and choices throughout the unit. Each task, activity, or assignment was viewed and analyzed through the lens of the standards. Every decision was based on promoting alignment with the content standards. This alignment provided a very deliberate and powerful tool for strengthening the instructional focus with the students. Each assessment task was rated according to its ability to reveal students' mathematical development.

The students must know and understand the content and performance standards. The criteria, or rubrics, that are used to evaluate students' work need to be clearly communicated to students. Throughout the unit, we analyzed pieces of students' work together for specific evidence of meeting the criteria.

How did the use of standards affect my instructional choices and the students' performance? The standards provided a framework for thinking about instructional experiences and the tasks that students should experience. This provided me with a more coherent perspective for the entire unit and caused me to use the content standards when considering the development of the students' understanding. The students reported that knowing my expectations helped them complete tasks and assessments in a more precise manner. They seemed to appreciate the specific feedback (self-evaluation and teacher evaluation) that comparing their work to the standards afforded. The potential for using content and performance standards to enhance instruction and student learning seems to be tremendous.

READ ABOUT...

Read about defining learning targets in "Breathe O_2 into Your Mathematics Program—Promote Openness and Ownership," by Gay Pitts (1997).

Read about defining performance standards in "More than Testing," by Elizabeth Badger (1992).

Blending Instruction and Assessment

READ ABOUT...

■ *Read about teachers trying to blend assessment and instruction in* A Collection of Math Lessons for Grades 3 through 6, *by Marilyn Burns (1990).*

■ *Read about blending instruction and assessment in "Linking Instruction and Assessment in the Mathematics Classroom," by Kay Sammons, Beth Kobett, Joan Heiss, and Francis (Skip) Fennell (1992); in "Seamless Assessment/Instruction = Good Teaching," by Diana Lambdin and Clare Forseth (1996); in "Connecting Learning and Teaching through Assessment," by Jean Moon (1993); and in "Integrating Assessment and Instruction," by Donald Chambers (1993).*

RESOURCES

For examples of good assessment practices in action, look at:

■ *WGBH videotapes on instruction and assessment*

■ *PBS Mathline videotapes*

We want to align our curriculum goals, instructional methods, and assessments. The NCTM *Curriculum and Evaluation Standards for School Mathematics* summarized the issue (p. 193):

> The assessment of students' mathematics learning should enable educators to draw conclusions about their instructional needs, their progress in achieving the goals of the curriculum, and the effectiveness of a mathematics program. The degree to which meaningful inferences can be drawn from such an assessment depends on the degree to which the assessment methods and tasks are aligned or are in agreement with the curriculum. Little information is produced about students' mastery of curricular topics when the assessment methods and tasks do not reflect curricular goals, objectives, and content; the instructional emphases of the mathematics program; or how the material is taught.

When instruction and assessment match, we find many benefits:

■ Expectations are clarified.

■ Fairness in assessment is assured.

■ Lessons and activities focus on learning results and outcomes.

■ The necessary adjustments in teaching can be made.

■ Assessment becomes part of learning rather than an interruption to learning.

CHAPTER *1*

The Importance of Assessment

In **figure 1.11** the comments from people in various walks of life reflect the importance of assessment and the need to blend it with instruction and the world outside the classroom.

FIG. 1.11

Getting Started

READ ABOUT...

■ *Read about a teacher's struggle in finding new ways to assess her elementary school students' work in "On-the-Job Learning" in* Mathematics Assessment: Cases and Discussion Questions for Grades K–5, *edited by William S. Bush (2001).*

■ *Read about a middle school teacher's attempt to try a new approach to instruction and assessment in "Does It Measure Up?" in* Mathematics Assessment: Cases and Discussion Questions for Grades 6–12, *edited by William S. Bush (2000, pp. 11–16).*

HOW SHALL I BEGIN?

Here are some suggestions from other teachers.

■ Pick *one* idea from this book and try it, then try another and another.

■ Don't try to do it all at once.

■ Work with other teachers to share ideas and agonies.

■ Start students in explaining and writing in mathematics early in the year.

■ Have them be sure to show all their work.

■ Ask them to work in groups and explain to each other how they worked on a problem. Have them make a group report about all the things they tried.

■ Ask them to describe what they did and explain why they are sure their answers are reasonable.

■ As you teach, practice asking questions of students. For example:

■ What do you need to do now?

■ How did you decide to do that?

■ What does the first sentence mean?

■ What is the problem asking you to do?

■ What numbers did you use?

■ Clarify standards and criteria with students, and refer to them frequently.

■ Persevere, even if changes feel awkward to you and the students at first.

CHAPTER *1*

Chapter 2

Selecting and Developing Tools for Assessment: What Are My Choices?

Teacher-to-Teacher

I have lots of questions about the tasks I can use. What makes a good assessment task? What do I want to find out, or what can I find out that I can't get with the assessment I use now? What are all these kinds of assessment we're talking about? What about technology?

Good Assessment Practices

WHAT IS GOOD ASSESSMENT?

A classroom assessment program must be useful to teachers, students, parents, and decision makers. To be useful, good assessment should—

- match what students have been studying;

- focus on important mathematics rather than the trivial;

- yield useful information, not just "scores";

- use clear and helpful criteria;

- provide a complete picture of students' learning and abilities;

- allow students to continue to learn mathematics during and after the assessment experience.

To judge the usefulness of an assessment task, we can ask ourselves questions such as these:

Is it about important mathematics?

The answer varies according to grade level and local programs or curricula. Once we know the topics to be included in the curriculum, we look at how students work with mathematics. For any topic, students may explore or may demonstrate that they can understand the concept, do the mathematics, arrive at a correct answer, and use the ideas to solve real problems.

An example of mathematics that may not be important at this level is the mastery of ratio and proportion concepts, which may still be developmental and exploratory. For more information about important mathematics, see the NCTM *Standards* books listed in the bibliography.

Can we get useful information for a variety of purposes?

- During preassessment, we might look for what students already know or do not know and try to identify their misconceptions.

- For ongoing instructional decisions, we may want to know where students are today. Assessment might be based on oral responses to questions asked by a teacher or another student, observations of students at work, or a daily review of work done.

- For periodic or end-of-unit assessment, we might want to be sure students have learned or mastered what is important. Assessment tools might include questions that cover the subject thoroughly, an oral report to the class, or a portfolio of the student's work.

- For summative or end-of-year district- or state-administered assessments, we might use a variety of methods that give a realistic and complete picture of students' progress.

Can we define criteria for success and communicate them to students?

The criteria for success should be clearly described but flexible enough to allow for unusual or unexpected responses. As teachers, we may expect a particular kind of answer yet find that the students' understanding can be different from ours and still acceptable. The opportunity for student creativity is usually an added benefit. Criteria for success can be described with general standards or rubrics or with specific descriptors for a particular task. Students and parents as well as teachers should have access to information about criteria. Otherwise, the assessment process is closed and secretive.

Can students learn from the assessment?

Our feedback to students from assessment can enhance their learning. In addition, assessment that engages and involves students in assessing their own learning can enhance learning still further. Throughout this book, you will find a thread of student self-assessment and student discussion of mathematics, with various kinds of feedback from teachers or peers, all of which can help students learn. In the past, students often have taken major tests without an opportunity to follow up with a discussion of the problems, to confirm their own success, or to identify the additional study they need to do. Good assessment must be part of the learning process.

WHAT SHOULD WE ASSESS?

The mathematics learned in the elementary school classroom provides the basis for future success in mathematics. With that in mind, we want to consider the balance of important mathematical topics, mathematical skills, learning processes, and possible uses of the results. Here are some of the important mathematical ideas and topics. (This list will change according to local requirements.) For each of these topics we want students to understand the concept and be able to do the work efficiently and correctly, explain their thinking, and apply a variety of strategies:

- Estimation
- Using measurement tools
- Basic facts
- Functions and algebraic ideas
- Probability and statistics concepts
- Making and interpreting many kinds of graphs
- Spatial reasoning in geometry

We might also want to assess the following mathematical skills:

- Finding correct or reasonable answers for simple problems
- Giving correct, automatic responses for basic facts
- Applying new skills in problems close to real life
- Applying previously learned skills to new problems
- Using appropriate strategies to solve problems
- Working through complex problems that may have more than one good response

In this chapter you will learn about—

- good assessment practices;
- tasks and open-ended questions;
- developing good assessment tasks;
- evaluating assessment tasks;
- questions, observations, interviews, and conferences;
- inventories and journals;
- tests and quizzes;
- portfolios and collections of work;
- technology and assessment.

Good Assessment Practices

READ ABOUT...

■ *Read about a teacher in grades 4–5 struggling with a variety of assessment approaches in "How Do I Assess Thee? Let Me Count the Ways..." in* Mathematics Assessment: Cases and Discussion Questions for Grades K–5, *edited by William S. Bush (2001).*

■ *Read about teachers deciding what to assess in "Make New Lessons, but Keep the Old: One Is Silver, the Other Is Gold," by Deborah Nieding (1998).*

Or, we can look for effective learning processes:

■ Engaging in a task, exhibiting persistence

■ Planning, organizing, and carrying out plans

■ Being flexibile, using alternatives if one plan doesn't work

■ Discussing and analyzing mathematical information

■ Clearly explaining and communicating

■ Self-assessing or self-correcting, revising

The results of our assessment will help us answer questions from students and their parents:

■ How am I doing?

■ How far have I gone toward my goals?

■ What have I learned?

■ Does my work meet the content and performance standards?

■ What additional instructional experiences are needed?

■ How can I improve my work?

■ Am I learning the math I need for next year and for the future?

■ What else do I want or need to do or learn?

■ What am I confused about?

WHAT KINDS OF ASSESSMENTS SHOULD I USE?

A variety of assessment tools or approaches are needed for a variety of situations. Some are already part of our daily classroom process. The seam between assessment and instruction or learning is for the most part invisible. For example, observation is and has been constant in any classroom. As a result of informal observation, a teacher may ask another question of the student, give new directions, or make any other instructional decision. Informally, the ebb and flow of classwork continues. A significant recent change is developing systematic ways to record and use the results of these observations. Another recent development is identifying tasks or activities to be used for assessment and explaining to students the standards or rubrics by which their performance will be judged. Below are brief descriptions of some of the kinds of assessment currently used by many teachers. Consider trying one thing at a time. The list is to help you, not to overwhelm you.

Tasks and Daily Work

Assessment does not have to be a separate effort. Sometimes we may want to select papers from the regular daily work to review and record as assessment. It might be the same assignment collected from all the students in a class or something special from an individual or a small group of students. In this case, there will be little or no difference between instructional tasks and assessment tasks. When assessment tasks come from a source other than daily classroom work, they should still be based on, and similar to, regular classroom work.

CHAPTER *2*

Good Assessment Practices

Open-Ended Questions

Asking open-ended questions is one of the easiest ways to begin changing instruction and assessment. An open-ended question is one that can be solved with more than one strategy and may have more than one solution. Students choose or create their own words, diagrams, graphs, or methods to represent their solutions.

Some teachers make a distinction between open-ended questions, which have many right answers, and open-middled questions, which have one right answer but allow many different strategies. Others believe that students should form a regular habit of looking for more than one strategy and being alert to the possibility of more than one answer.

The degree of openness varies according to the purpose. For example, if we want to see whether students can set up a division problem, we say, "What is 365 divided by 20?" If we want to find out whether they can organize data, we give them the data in rough form and ask them to organize it. We frequently ask students to explain or defend their reasoning.

Observations and Questioning

Most of us, as we observe students working on tasks, have a pretty good idea of what they have learned. Listening to students as they work in groups can be especially revealing. We usually need to ask a few questions to get insight into their thinking: "How did you decide which strategy to try?" "What was your reasoning for this part?" "If you did it again, what else would you try?" and so on. We emphasize the use of questions to encourage students to do their own thinking. Asking questions can be more productive than telling students what to do and how to do it.

When we record some of these observations, the results can be used for formal purposes, such as grades and parent conferences, as well as for instructional decisions. We regularly observe participation and oral reports in most class-rooms. A formal assessment might include a checklist or evaluation sheet that outlines what is expected; students could use it in planning and teachers could use it in assessing.

Interviews and Conferences

We may want to schedule regular one-on-one or small-group meetings with students to find out more about their learning. The questions used in whole-class discussions are also useful in interviews. An interview gives us a chance to find out what thinking is behind the written work.

Journals, Inventories, and Logs

Many teachers have students keep journals of their mathematics work. Journals are a good way to understand students' thinking and communicate with students about their work as it progresses. Inventories allow students to report beliefs, attitudes, and progress concisely. Even a simple daily log of what work was completed can keep us informed.

Good Assessment Practices

Projects and Investigations

Longer projects and investigations offer assessment opportunities of all kinds: interviews, observations, ongoing work, oral reports, and culminating activities. An important aspect of long-term work is students' opportunity to evaluate their progress and revise or refine their work. We have an opportunity to assess how well students plan and organize and how well they work with others.

Portfolios

A portfolio collection of work, usually selected with guidelines, is one of the best ways to look at students' progress over time. Portfolios give us a chance to assess students' strengths and capture their mathematical power.

Tests, Quizzes, and Short-Answer Questions

Tests and quizzes have been the standard forms of classroom assessment. In the past, they have tended to focus on mastery and retention. New types of tests and quizzes ask more-probing questions with directions to elaborate or explain the answers. A multiple-choice question, for example, might now ask students to explain why they chose the answer they did. Part of the reason for doing so is to discourage students from blindly choosing an answer.

Group Tests

Because many of us have students work in groups, it makes sense to design special group tests. They might use problems that relate to what the students have been studying but are more challenging than those assigned for seatwork or homework. Students will have to consult with one another and think through a problem. A group's grade may come from any member's paper or explanation, so the group must be sure that everyone understands.

On-Demand Assessment

The term *on-demand* refers to tests required by the school administration or by a state or province on a particular date, with the test coming from some outside source. Standardized tests are an example of on-demand testing. Kentucky, for example, includes open-ended questions and multiple-choice items as part of its state on-demand assessment.

Tasks and Open-Ended Questions

HOW AND WHERE CAN I GET GOOD ASSESSMENT TASKS?

It is often difficult to find good tasks and questions that align with our instruction. In this section we include some strategies for finding, revising, and creating tasks and open-ended questions. We may not have to look very far because one of the best sources may be material that is already in the curriculum or program. Here are some examples.

Add a Probing Question or Change an Old Problem

All we may have to do is add another question or two that reveal students' thinking. Students as well as teachers can gain understanding from new kinds of questions. For example, **figure 2.1** offers a conventional problem. If we add one more instruction, "Explain how you found your answer," we can get a much better picture of students' understanding, as well as help them form the habit of thinking about what they are doing instead of guessing or rushing for answers.

FIG. 2.1

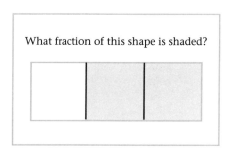

We can also change the problem's features. For example, if we direct students to draw a line across the shape, we can ask what fraction of the new figure is shaded (see **fig. 2.2**). Different students will probably offer different responses, which presents a good opportunity for discussion and may offer an opportunity to develop the idea of equivalent fractions.

FIG. 2.2

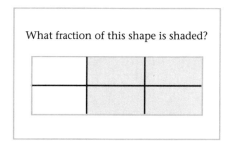

We may want to brainstorm and keep handy some good questions to use for extending problems and tasks. Even when textbooks have developed this kind of questioning, we will still need to vary the questions as we watch students work. Every situation may be different.

Here are a few questions to start the list:

- Is there a pattern? How could you describe it?
- What is different and what is the same?
- What other change could you make?
- What have you seen before that looked like this?
- What is the difference between your answer and those of others in your group?
- Are there other ways to get the answer?
- What did you do to check your answer?
- How do you know your answer is correct?
- How would you explain your answer to someone else?

Tasks and Open-Ended Questions

Ask for Explanations

Pull out an old true-or-false quiz. Ask the students to discuss it and give reasons why they believe each statement is true or false. If the questions permit, ask students to use manipulatives, diagrams, numbers, or other ways to illustrate their points. One more step is to ask the students to rewrite the false statements to make them true or perhaps to rewrite the true statements to make them false. This strategy can be used as a group assessment as well as an individual assignment.

Use the News

Newspapers and magazines are excellent sources for tasks and open-ended questions.

- Weather reports

  - Look at the weather map. Where is it raining today? Where is it hotter than it is here?

  - What patterns of weather does our town have?

  - Where else is the weather the same as it is here?

  - How would you figure out how long the sun will shine tomorrow?

- Elections

  - How many people are likely to be voting in this election?

  - If somebody has to get 50 percent of the votes to win, about how many would that be?

  - What if several people are running for the same office?

  - Take polls of which candidates people think they will vote for, and display the results in a graph.

- Sports statistics

  - How many more runs did one baseball team score than another? Which teams are ahead in winning games for the year? Make graphs of team records.

  - Do the fastest runners run in the longest races? What are some records for different kinds of races? Why are they different? (Have an almanac handy for these questions.)

- Interesting articles about animals

  - Draw maps of where animals are found. How far away are they from here?

Make Connections with Other Subjects

In social studies, you might try these activities:

- Use your own or others' travel records. Put up or distribute copies of a map of where you (or an imaginary person) went for a vacation. Ask the students to use the map scale to try to calculate how many miles you traveled. Ask them how far apart the cities you visited are.

CHAPTER *2*

Tasks and Open-Ended Questions

■ Compare the sizes or shapes of homes in different countries.

■ Make time lines of historical events, or time lines of students' own lives.

In literature, you might try these activities:

■ Use books and have students draw diagrams or use maps to accompany the stories.

■ Have students draw graphs that depict word length, frequency of particular letters, or frequency of particular words.

■ Have students create word problems related to a story.

Share with Other Teachers

Sharing and discussing assessment with others can make it a lot easier. We can exchange ideas about what we see our students learn and how we know they have learned. Working together will increase not only the number of assessment questions and tasks we collect but also our understanding of the information gained from them. If two of us use the same tasks with our students, we can compare the results and get ideas for instructional decisions.

Collect Neighborhood or School Data

Use neighborhood and school data as a source of original activities and questions. Have students organize the data, make a graph or diagram if possible, and ask their own questions. Refer to school events:

■ We are having an assembly today. How many students are in this class (or the school) and how much space will we take up?

■ What kind of fences do we have in this area? How many of each? Of how many different colors?

■ What size are the shoes that most students in our school wear?

Opportunities That Arise during the Day

Use everyday occurrences; for example, if you use paper cups for a class lunch, ask the students to count the number of paper cups used and decide how many would be needed if there were a class lunch every week.

Mathematics Conferences

At a conference, go to as many sessions as possible and don't overlook the publishers' exhibits. More useful and interesting books are available now than ever before.

Professional Journals and Publications

The National Council of Teachers of Mathematics journals *Teaching Children Mathematics* and *Mathematics Teaching in the Middle School* are outstanding sources of material for curriculum and assessment.

READ ABOUT...

■ *Read about an elementary school teacher who poses an open-ended task to her students in "The Power of the Blank Page" in* Mathematics Assessment: Cases and Discussion Questions for Grades K–5, *edited by William S. Bush (2001).*

■ *Read about a teacher who struggles to create tasks for her elementary school students in "Primary Portfolios" in* Mathematics Assessment: Cases and Discussion Questions for Grades K–5, *edited by William S. Bush (2001).*

■ *Read about developing open-ended questions in "Assessing Open-Ended Problems," by Kathleen Conway (1999).*

Tasks and Open-Ended Questions

READ ABOUT...

■ *Read about a sixth-grade teacher who is concerned that the task she gave her students is too open in "Open Car Wash" in* Mathematics Assessment: Cases and Discussion Questions for Grades 6–12, *edited by William S. Bush (2000).*

HOW OPEN SHOULD TASKS BE?

Questions should be open enough so that students take some responsibility for planning and carrying out their strategies but not so "unformed" that they are baffling and prevent students from knowing where to start. We learn by experience what will work with our students.

When students have had experience with somewhat open-ended problems, they will have more strategies available. We may want to tell students that we are looking to see whether they can choose a starting strategy or that we are looking to see whether they can choose the right tools. **Figure 2.3** is an example of a structured problem that might be used at the beginning of the year. A more open problem for later in the year is shown in **figure 2.4**. The second problem requires students to be the decision makers about which measurements should be considered, which should be reported, and what tools to use. They may talk about area, length of sides, height, angles, diagonals, or other differences. This kind of problem provides us an opportunity to observe students' abilities to think of strategies, to carry out a plan, and to organize information.

FIG. 2.3

A Structured Problem

How much bigger is the large rectangular region than the small one?

My estimate is _____.

Use a ruler to measure the sides of each rectangle. Write the numbers next to the sides of the rectangles.

What is the area of each? Write it inside the rectangle.

How much bigger is the large rectangle? _____

CHAPTER 2

Tasks and Open-Ended Questions

FIG. 2.4

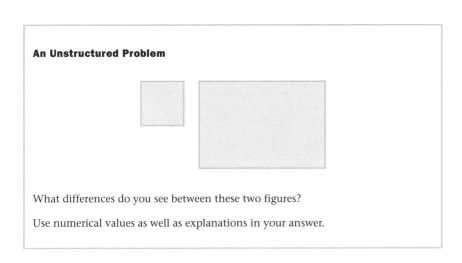

An Unstructured Problem

What differences do you see between these two figures?

Use numerical values as well as explanations in your answer.

Teachers with some experience in developing and using open-ended tasks have suggested the questions in "Tips from Teachers" on this page to help others plan for the use of good tasks.

Developing Good Assessment Tasks

READ ABOUT...

■ *Read about developing good tasks in "Catering to All Abilities through 'Good' Questions," by Peter Sullivan and David Clarke (1991), and in "Using Performance Assessment to Determine Mathematical Dispositions," by Judith Collison (1992).*

Figure 2.5 provides steps to follow in order to create, evaluate, and use a task for assessment. Note that this procedure is primarily an assessment of the task itself, with students' work used as part of the process.

FIG. 2.5

Steps in the Task-Development Process	Evaluating the Task
Consider the **topic** to be assessed.	Is it appropriate for the students' level? Do the students have the prerequisite understanding or skills?
Choose a **task**, problem, or investigation.	Is the problem open enough to accommodate a variety of styles and understanding?
Create the first draft of **criteria**. What will it mean to do good work?	Do the students understand the qualities of complete good work? Have they seen examples?
Discuss the problem with the students.	Can the students understand the situation?
Have the students begin **work** on the problem.	Does the problem engage students? Do groups work together? Are resources available?
Have the students present or turn in **first drafts** or reports on the problem.	Did the students understand what to do? What needs to be changed, improved, or added? Was the problem rich enough or could more be added? Are there possible extensions?
Clarify and explain the criteria.	Have the students found unexpected avenues? Are the criteria complete and adequate?
Continue to review students' work to correct flaws in the task.	Does the students' work reflect the criteria? Should we make new versions of the problem?
Compare responses to the criteria—use rubrics, discussions, self-assessment, reports, interviews, etc.	Does this task lead students to— ■ show understanding? ■ complete all work? ■ look at all options and find more than one approach and more than one response? ■ go beyond the original expectations of the task?
Consider the next **topic** to be assessed.	

CHAPTER 2

Evaluating Assessment Tasks

To help us select or define a good task, we might want to try out the assessment strategy of devising a set of criteria, or a rubric. (See chapter 4 for more information about standards, criteria, and rubrics.) Here's a possible start, however, with room for you to add characteristics.

An effective or good task should have these qualities:

- *Mathematics*. It is about important mathematics.

- *Appropriateness*. It matches whatever mathematics we have been studying and the developmental level of the students.

- *Skills*. It lets students use their learned skills at their own level of understanding.

- *Presentation*. It clearly states the problem without confusion. It is not tricky. Information is presented both in words and in format in an understandable way. The directions are clear.

- *Thinking*. It is open to several ways of thinking about the problem. It leads students to show how they think, not just to write down the final answer. It gives only necessary directions, letting students make decisions wherever possible.

- *Context*. It uses contexts that are interesting and understandable to students and that allow students to relate mathematics to real life.

- *Other descriptors of a good task*:

_____

_____

_____

_____

_____

Evaluating Assessment Tasks

New Standards, a joint program of the National Center on Education and the Economy and the Learning Research and Development Center at the University of Pittsburgh (1997), developed a useful set of criteria to judge appropriate tasks for students (see **fig. 2.6**).

FIG. 2.6

New Standards™ Task Design Guidelines

- Use language, context, and audience that are accessible and familiar to students.
  - Provide a context that does not require specialized knowledge.
  - Keep language as simple and jargon-free as possible.
  - Include tasks with visual clues (pictures or diagrams) and words to clarify.

- Provide students with an audience and a role to play within the problem situation.
  - Set the standard for mathematical communication.
  - Make the purpose of the task apparent to students in a realistic way.
  - Tap into students' interests.
  - Give students opportunities to make decisions or express points of view that can be supported with mathematical reasoning.

- Create a task that has an authentic relationship to its context.
  - Use "real life" situations that allow for realistic reasoning.
  - Find tasks that promote the use of a variety of mathematical models, tools, and resources.

- Make tasks accessible but well differentiated.
  - Find tasks that give all students a chance to enter the task and show positive achievement.
  - Find tasks that are not limiting to less mathematically sophisticated students.
  - Find tasks that give all students opportunities to think and reason about important mathematical ideas.

- Do not provide too much structure.
  - Find a balance between "structure" and "openness" (overstructuring can fragment tasks, and providing too much guidance can limit students' opportunities to think for themselves).
  - Choose a mathematically rich situation that helps students make connections using essential mathematics.
  - Provide an easy example (thus "using up" the trivial response).
  - Show an incorrect method and ask students to state why it's incorrect.
  - Include a response to a different task requiring the same type of product.

From *New Standards Performance Standards* (National Center on Education and the Economy and University of Pittsburgh 1997, p.167). Reprinted with permission.

CHAPTER 2

Evaluating Assessment Tasks

The following issues might also be considered in selecting existing tasks, adapting old tasks, or creating new tasks:

- *Purpose of the task.* Is it intended to be an end-of-unit, cumulative assessment, or is it to be used to determine how well students are developing an understanding of a new concept?

- *Revision.* Should students have a chance to revise this work before we score it? Should they revise it after we have scored it? How would doing so enhance their learning? Would the task still be valid as an assessment task? Revision can give students the opportunity to produce work that meets the criteria or rubric. Feedback from the teacher, suggestions from peers, and the process of analyzing work to help it meet expectations can lead to improved communication, correct computational work, and a clearer understanding of concepts. Students might be asked to revise particular pieces of work but probably not every one.

- *Challenging tasks.* Talk with students about how they see expectations change as tasks become more challenging. Being able to assess their own work should help them develop an interest in mathematics. We may want to work with students to revise standards or rubrics as the year goes by.

- *Record keeping.* How is the recording going? Is it too cumbersome; does it need to be simplified? Are we able to interpret it for grades, parent conferences, and so on? Think about cutting down on records so that the focus will be on what is really important or so that you have to think about only one or two ideas to assess for each day or week.

READ ABOUT...

■ *Read about* revising assessment tasks in *"Polishing a Data Task: Seeking Better Assessment,"* by Judith Zawojewski (1996).

Questions, Observations, Interviews, and Conferences

Talking with students is the primary avenue to good assessment. We sit down and listen to a group discuss a problem and ask them questions, make comments, suggest new materials to use, and so on. We talk with individual students, informally or formally. We constantly observe students as they work.

WHAT KINDS OF QUESTIONS CAN WE ASK DURING AN OBSERVATION OR INTERVIEW?

Asking questions is an art. Some of us seem to know exactly what question will give us the most information or help students get started with their work, but many of us need to prepare questions ahead of time. Good questions might—

■ elicit information about where the students are in their learning;

■ help the students review what they have done;

■ help the students focus on their next steps;

■ encourage the students to discuss what they are doing;

■ refine the students' communication skills.

Below is a starter list of questions to try.

Focus on What the Problem Says

■ What information does the first part of the problem give you? The second part?

■ Can you put that into your own words?

■ How is this problem like others we have done before?

■ What kind of mathematics is in this problem?

Check for Estimation

■ Did you make an estimate?

■ How could an estimate help you know if you are right?

■ Could you make a guess and check to see if it works?

Questions, Observations, Interviews, and Conferences

Look at the Problem-Solving Process

- What have you already tried?

- Have you tried using manipulatives to show the parts of the problem?

- What if you worked backward?

- What do you need to do next?

Ask about Communication and Cooperation

- Can you explain to the rest of your group what you are doing?

- Have you checked your idea with others?

- How did your group use ideas from each person?

- Where could you go for more information?

Look for Organization

- Is there a pattern?

- How did you or could you organize the information?

- Would a diagram or chart help?

- What if you changed this part of the problem?

Encourage Students to Look Back

- How could you check your work?

- Do you think there could be a different answer?

- Is there more than one possible correct answer?

- Is this your best work? Would you like to revise it?

READ ABOUT...

- *Read about creating good questions in "Modifying Our Questions to Assess Students' Thinking," by Michaele F. Chappell and Denisse R. Thompson (1999), and in "Assessing through Questioning," by Mary Montgomery Lindquist (1988).*

- *Read about asking good questions to uncover students' thinking in "Assessing Children's Reasoning: It's an Age-Old Problem," by Jacque Smith (1996), and in "Understanding Children's Reasoning," by George Bright (1996).*

Questions, Observations, Interviews, and Conferences

WHAT SHOULD I CONSIDER IN MAKING OBSERVATIONS?

Effective assessment involves ongoing, consistent, and focused observations. For a complete picture, we observe students at different times of the day, in different settings, doing different kinds of work. We record what is actually seen and heard. The diagram in **figure** 2.7 suggests some of the things we might observe in students.

FIG. 2.7

Observations reveal more than whether a student has a correct or incorrect answer.

CHAPTER 2

Questions, Observations, Interviews, and Conferences

WHAT TYPES OF DOCUMENTATION MIGHT I USE FOR OBSERVATIONS?

Most observation will be unstructured, a regular part of the classroom action. Sometimes a special purpose might require more-structured observations. In either instance, documentation is a key to accumulating information about students' learning. It is also one of the most important changes in assessment. Most of us have made mental notes of our observations but have seldom made more-formal efforts to validate the observations through recording what we see. **Figure** 2.8 gives some differences between structured and unstructured observations.

FIG. 2.8

Structured observation—	Unstructured observation—
▓ involves assigning a specific task;	▓ involves observing tasks as they occur naturally;
▓ is done at a specific time in a specific setting;	▓ is done at any time in any setting;
▓ becomes the focus of the lesson;	▓ becomes an integral part of the lesson;
▓ provides a snapshot of the students;	▓ provides a broader picture of the student;
▓ usually involves observing all students;	▓ may involve observing only a few students;
▓ if overdone, may become a documentation nightmare.	▓ makes documentation easier to manage.

Questions, Observations, Interviews, and Conferences

TIPS FROM TEACHERS

■ *Documentation is vital to making observations useful.*

■ *No one can remember everything that is seen and heard.*

■ *Documentation should reflect what is seen, without judgments.*

■ *Documentation may include questions about points to ponder later.*

■ *Observation and documentation skills will develop through practice.*

Below are some examples of documentation methods and tools. Other examples can be found in chapter 3.

Documentation Methods

- Jottings
- Anecdotal records
- Narratives
- Running records

Documentation Tools

- Index cards
- Class checklists
- Self-stick notes
- Mailing labels or computer labels
- Monthly calendars
- Notebooks
- Recording devices
- Computers

AN OBSERVATION EXAMPLE

Ms. Hardy wanted to find out how much her students knew about geometric shapes and area. She divided the class into groups and gave each group a set of thirty color tiles. The first task was to use the tiles to make all the different-sized squares they could and record them on graph paper. Before they started, she asked them to discuss with the group what they thought the largest square would be. As they discussed, she listened.

She heard one group decide that a square could be any shape as long as no tiles were sticking out. She made a note to bring up the definition of a square in class discussion.

Another group moved right to mathematics because they said, "We know that $5 \times 6 = 30$," and they began to make a list of all the number sentences for thirty. Ms. Hardy put a check beside the note about defining a square, adding the word rectangle.

Questions, Observations, Interviews, and Conferences

AN OBSERVATION EXAMPLE (continued)

In a few minutes, Ms. Hardy called the class together. Her first question was "What is a square?" The students responded, "All the sides are the same," "It has four corners," "It has four sides." She then asked for a definition of a rectangle. The responses were the same, so she asked, "What is the difference between a rectangle and a square?" As students volunteered, she asked them to come to the chalkboard and draw the shapes they were talking about.

When she felt that students understood the square and rectangle concepts, she sent them back to groups to continue their work. Both groups she had observed quickly corrected their misconceptions and successfully found all the squares, from a one-by-one square up to a five-by-five square.

There was some discussion about what to do with the remaining five tiles, but when Ms. Hardy noticed that one group had made them into a two-by-two square and a one-by-one square, she complimented them and asked them to explain their thinking to the class.

TYPICAL OBSERVATION SCENARIOS

■ Observe while interacting with students.

Ms. Dorree's class is using bingo chips to make multiplication arrays. As the students build each array and record the multiplication problem on a slate, she is able to circulate through the room, help students, and make jottings or anecdotal notes on the clipboard. She may add details later.

■ Observe when not interacting with students.

Using sale flyers, calculators, and recording sheets, Mr. David's class is working in cooperative groups on buying several items. As the students work and discuss, he moves around the room, briefly observing each group's interactions and writing down information before assisting the group or calling the class together for a discussion.

■ Observe students during the day and document information when they are out of the room.

Ms. Lissam's class is making fraction books in order to visualize division of a whole item. The students are folding and cutting strips then labeling them with the correct fraction. She finds that she can only circulate around the room and assist students. Documentation at this point is intrusive. She makes mental notes as she circulates. After the students leave, she is able to write down information on the basis of her mental notes and the students' work. She realizes that she must be careful to record only factual information. Any judgments or opinion she has will be written in the form of a question.

READ ABOUT...

■ *Read about teachers who use observation to assess their students in "On-the-Job Learning" in* Mathematics Assessment: Cases and Discussion Questions for Grades K–5, *edited by William S. Bush (2001), and "Tessellation Presentation" in* Mathematics Assessment: Cases and Discussion Questions for Grades 6–12, *edited by Willliam S. Bush (2000).*

■ *Read about how teachers use observation to assess students in* A Collection of Math Lessons from Grades 3 through 6, *by Marilyn Burns (1990).*

■ *Read about observing students in "Walking Around: Getting More from Informal Assessment," by Karen A. Cole (1999).*

Questions, Observations, Interviews, and Conferences

WHAT ARE THE BENEFITS OF INTERVIEWS AND CONFERENCES?

Interviews and conferences help us refine the information from observations. **Figure 2.9** gives some of the benefits.

FIG. 2.9

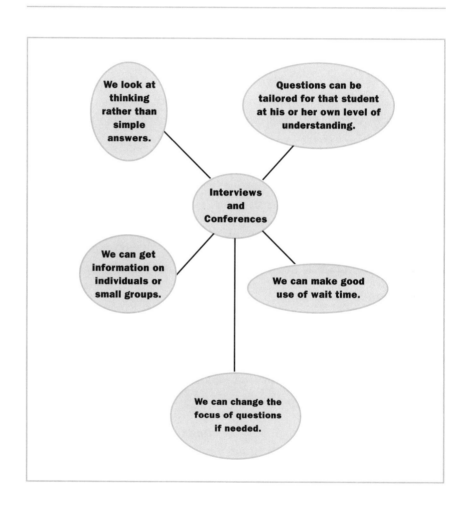

Questions, Observations, Interviews, and Conferences

HOW DO INTERVIEWS AND CONFERENCES DIFFER?

A conference is like a conversation and can be broad in scope. Conferences are useful for getting information about students' general progress and for suggesting some directions to take. Here is an example of a conference:

Mr. Pierson and Logan met during recess. Mr. Pierson wanted to find out how Logan was progressing on his problem of the week. The problem asked the students to find at least six different ways to show the fraction three-fourths and explain each method. Logan seemed to be having trouble with the explanations.

Mr. P.:	What did you use first to show the fraction?
Logan:	I used a grid sheet and colored in three-fourths.
Mr. P.:	How did you know it was three-fourths?
Logan:	I drew lines to divide the grid into four equal parts and colored in three.
Mr. P.:	Sounds reasonable. See if you can write down what you just said. (*Logan writes down his explanation.*)
Mr. P.:	What else did you use?
Logan:	I used eight blocks—six red and two blue.
Mr. P.:	Why did you use eight blocks?
Logan:	Because I could make fourths out of eight. Every two blocks is a fourth.
Mr. P.:	What do the colors mean?
Logan:	Well, the red means three-fourths and the blue means one-fourth.
Mr. P.:	Could you have used any other number of blocks?
Logan:	Sure, I could have used four, but that would have been too easy. I guess I could use sixteen or some other numbers, too.
Mr. P.:	Would ten have worked?
Logan:	Hmm (*looks at blocks, thinking*). No, I don't think so, because if I divided them into four fourths, there would still be some left. Two left.

Mr. Pierson continued to ask Logan to explain his methods. Logan still needed two more, but he had three more days to work on the problem. Mr. Pierson suggested he think about all the materials they had used during the year.

Logan asked if he could come in again if the explanations were still not working. Mr. Pierson and Logan agreed to meet again two days later.

Questions, Observations, Interviews, and Conferences

READ ABOUT...

■ *Read about how teachers used interviews and conferences to uncover students' errors and misconceptions in "The New Student," "Melanie's Place-Value Understanding," and "When the Wrong Way Works" in* Mathematics Assessment: Cases and Discussion Questions for Grades K–5, *edited by William S. Bush (2001).*

■ *Read about conducting interviews in "What Can a Teacher Learn about a Pupil's Thinking through Oral Interviews?" by Francis Lankford, Jr. (1992), and in "Informing Learning through the Clinical Interview," by Madeleine J. Long and Meir Ben-Hur.*

An interview is more planned than a conference and can yield specific information about how a student approaches a task or what the student understands. It can reveal qualities about the student as an individual. For a successful interview, a set of specific questions should be prepared ahead of time.

Interviews may be formal or informal. They may take place during a scheduled time (recess, lunch, before or after school) or during the day while the rest of the class is working. Interviews can be conducted throughout the year. Students' responses may be recorded on an interview form that includes the questions or on any documentation tool that is already being used. The information may be used to diagnose and remediate or to plan enrichment experiences. In either case, probing questions will clarify and enhance observations.

As with most other assessments, time should be left for exploring other questions as they arise during the discussion. **Figure 2.10** offers an example of a set of general questions that a teacher might use in an interview. The advantages of preparing questions ahead of time are as follows:

■ We can think ahead of time about what we really need to know and what will be most helpful to the student.

■ We have a record of the questions asked and need only jot down the responses.

■ We ensure asking the same information of all students.

FIG. 2.10

Interview-Question Form

Student's name _____ Date _____

Task:

1. What have you done so far?

2. Is there any part of the task that is unclear?

3. What are your next steps?

4. Are there any additional resources or help that you need?

5. How could you extend this particular problem?

6. Other Notes:

CHAPTER *2*

Questions, Observations, Interviews, and Conferences

Some interviews, especially those used for diagnostic purposes, are more structured. **Figure 2.11** shows an example from the *Diagnostic Mathematics Program: Elementary* (Alberta Education 1990). This particular selection is from the problem-solving section. On the following page is a copy of a Student Profile from this program.

FIG. 2.11

Problem A

Magnifying Glass	$9.00
Butterfly Net	$4.00

Pam and her friends (7 in all) **each** want a magnifying glass. Every Saturday, **together** they can earn $14.00. How long will it take them to earn enough money to buy the magnifying glasses?

Understanding the Problem

1. In your own words, what does the problem ask?
2. This problem gives information about how many people?
3. How many magnifying glasses do they want to buy?
4. Does the problem tell how much each girl earns?
5. What information do we NOT need to answer the problem?

Developing and Carrying Out the Plan

6. How would you start to solve this problem?
7. What would you do to find this step? Carry out this plan.
8. Are you finished solving the problem?
9. Now what would you do?
10. Carry out this plan.
11. What is the answer to the problem?
12. How would you check your work to prove that your answer is correct?

Looking Back

13. Answer the question in a sentence.
14. Is your answer reasonable or unreasonable?

Looking Ahead

15. If the price of the magnifying glasses went up to $10.00 each, would the amount of time it takes to earn enough money differ? Explain.
16. Suppose Pam and her friends had to have the magnifying glasses for a science experiment in 4 weeks. How much would they have to earn each week to be able to buy the magnifying glasses?
17. Suppose Pam and her friends earned $18 per week, how long would it take them to earn enough money to buy the magnifying glasses?

Reproduced with permission of the Minister of Education, Province of Alberta, Canada, 1998.

Questions, Observations, Interviews, and Conferences

The Student Profile in **figure 2.12** from the problem-solving section of the *Diagnostic Mathematics Program: Elementary* (Alberta Education 1990) provides another example of a form that can be used for formal interviews with students.

FIG. 2.12

Student Profile

Name _____

Grade 5

Problem Solving

	Observation Checklist					In-Depth Evaluation		
	Strong	Adequate	Weak	Not Enough Information	Comments	Structured Interviews	Written Stage-Specific	All-Inclusive
UNDERSTANDING THE PROBLEM						P01 – 5	P02 – 5	P06 – 5
Attending/Analyzing/Associating								
Understands the words or phrases.								
Knows the question asked.								
Finds the given information.								
Knows what is needed information.								
Knows what is missing information.								
Knows the extraneous information.								
Restates the problem in own words.								
Interprets pictures and diagrams.								
DEVELOPING AND CARRYING OUT THE PLAN						P01 – 5	P03 – 5 S	P06 – 5
Synthesizing (S)								
Finds subproblems and solves.								
Selects appropriate strategies.								
Explains the plan.							M	
Finds the correct answer.								
Monitoring (M)								
Finds subproblems and checks steps.								
Checks the steps in doing the strategy.							C	
Reviews the steps taken.								
Combined Scores (C)								
LOOKING BACK						P01 – 5	P04 – 5	P06 – 5
Synthesizing								
Answers in a sentence the question asked.								
Restates the problem with the solution.								
Monitoring								
Checks reasonableness of answers.								
LOOKING AHEAD						P01 – 5	P05 – 5	
Synthesizing								
Does similar problems.								
Alters the problems and finds the effect.								
Generalizes the solution.								
COMBINED STAGES						P01 – 5		P06 – 5

CHAPTER 2

Inventories and Journals

WHAT CAN INVENTORIES AND JOURNALS ASSESS EFFECTIVELY?

The attitudes of students toward mathematics often affect their learning. It is important for us as teachers to assess attitudes on a regular basis and for students themselves to reflect on this aspect of their work. For example, a remark that a student "hates homework" may indicate a need for clearer directions for homework, for a different kind of assignment, or for contacting a parent to help resolve the problem. Inventories and journals are good sources of information about attitudes.

An informal interest inventory might be used at the beginning of the year to assess students' attitudes toward learning and mathematics, then be repeated later in the year to see if attitudes have changed. Journal prompts help with students' reflection and mathematical communication. Used as a follow-up to a mathematical experience, journal writing gives us additional information about a student's learning, which may not have been shown by previous questions and answers. Inventories, journals, and reflective questions can help us plan for conferences and interviews with students, suggesting specific questions we can ask.

Possible journal prompts include the following:

- By doing this problem, I have learned that …

- I used math to solve this problem by …

- I liked solving this problem because …

- I did not like solving this problem because …

- The hardest part was …

- The easiest part was …

- I was surprised that …

- I got started by …

- If I changed this problem, …

- I found another solution by …

- I got stuck on (or at) …

- When I got stuck, I did …

- When I drew a diagram of a problem, it …

- Today I found a pattern in …

Inventories and Journals

READ ABOUT...

▧ *Read about student journals in "I Thik the Cintanre will Hoder Lase: Journal Keeping in the Mathematics Class," by Sonia Helton (1995); in "Journal Writing: An Insight into Students' Understanding," by Karen Norwood and Glenda Carter (1994); in "Pic-Jour Math: Pictorial Journal Writing in Mathematics," by Andi Stix (1994); and in "Exploring Middle Graders' Mathematical Thinking through Journals," by Mary Lou DiPillo, Robert Sovchik, and Barbara Moss (1997).*

Figure 2.13 shows a simple mathematics inventory for younger students.

FIG. 2.13

MATH INTEREST INVENTORY

Name _____ Date _____

For each statement, mark the face that matches yours. Add comments if you wish.

This Is How I Feel About—

1. Math class
2. Volunteering to answer in math class
3. Being called on to answer
4. Working alone in math class
5. Working with a partner
6. Working with a group
7. Doing math homework
8. Having someone help me with math
9. Helping someone else in math
10. Learning something new in math
11. Addition and subtraction
12. Multiplication
13. Division
14. Using manipulatives
15. Drawing diagrams
16. Playing games of math
17. Explaining how I solve problems
18. Writing about math

19. _____

20. _____

Inventories and Journals

WHAT DO I CONSIDER IN READING JOURNAL ENTRIES BY STUDENTS?

It is important that we analyze journal entries carefully. **Figure 2.14** shows an example from the journal of one student, Scott. In this entry, Scott explains why he selected a particular number box (see **fig. 2.15**) to include in his portfolio. His teacher wrote the following reflections about Scott's work:

> I've found that asking about the assignment is important because misunderstandings lead to incorrect work. Scott obviously understood what to do. Of the various assignments we have done this report period, Scott felt this one had the most correct work. He knows that the division needs to be corrected and will continue to try it. How about that "hardest thing" comment!

READ ABOUT...

■ *Read about using inventories in "On the Nature of Teaching and Assessing 'Mathematical Power' and 'Mathematical Thinking,'" by Jonathan Jay Greenwood (1993).*

FIG. 2.14

Name _Scott_

Date _____

The assignment was to _give as many different ways of showing the number 79._

I selected this number box because _I did the most on it. It had only three wrong._

By doing number boxes, I have learned that _there are many ways of doing number boxes. I'm learning Roman numerals._

The hardest thing about number boxes is _when you can't think of anything to do on the number boxes_

Two things I will try to include in my next number box are _division and bigger multiplication._

Inventories and Journals

TIPS FROM TEACHERS

When we look at students' inventories or journals, we consider the following:

- *What can I learn about this student from these responses?*
- *What other questions would I ask in a conference or interview?*
- *Do the student's comments agree with my own observations?*
- *Does this student have a good idea of his or her own progress?*
- *What could I discuss with parents on the basis of this information?*
- *Is this a change from the student's past attitudes?*
- *Are these attitudes reflected in the quality of the student's daily work?*

FIG. 2.15

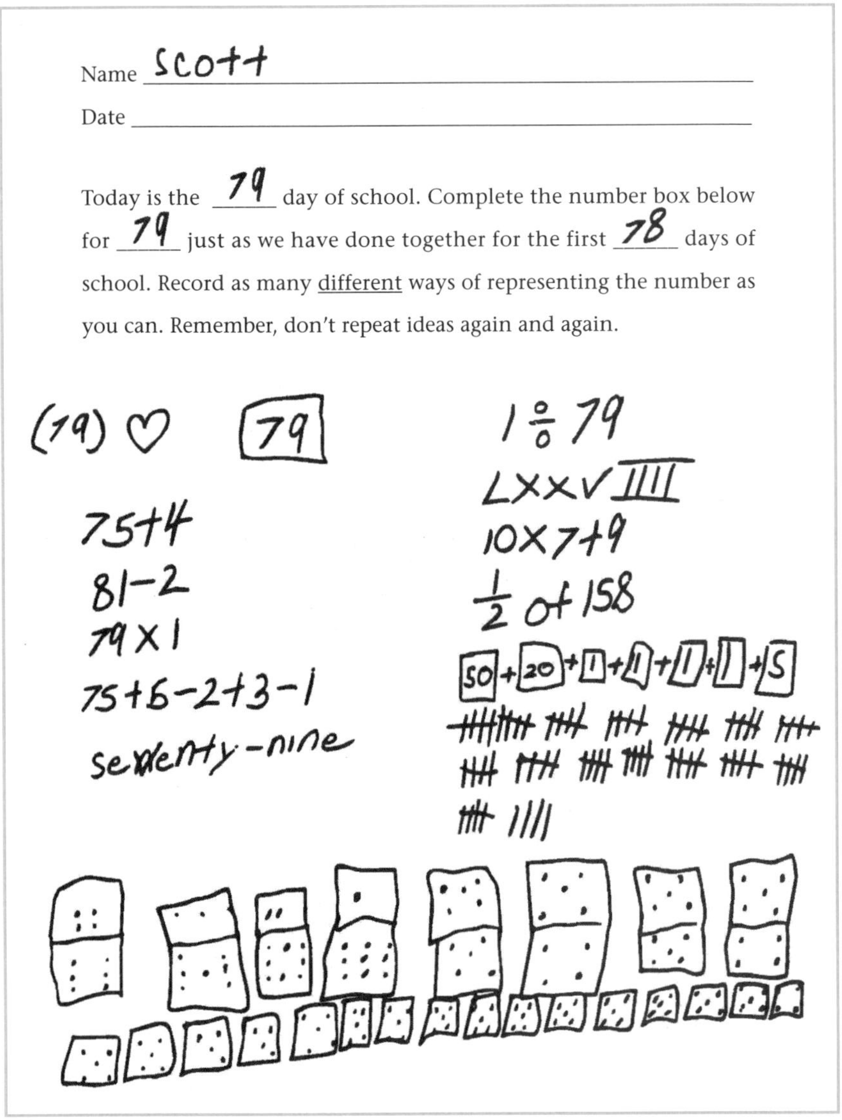

Name Scott

Date

Today is the 79 day of school. Complete the number box below for 79 just as we have done together for the first 78 days of school. Record as many different ways of representing the number as you can. Remember, don't repeat ideas again and again.

The teacher also reflected on Scott's work:

> *Although we hadn't talked about writing division problems yet, Scott had an idea of how to do one. I was surprised he could do a mixed problem using multiplication. He explained to me that he figured out the dice by counting by fives. "Fifteen sets of five got me to seventy-five, then I just needed four more for seventy-nine." He then explained to me that he had figured out the dominoes using tens. "I need seven groups of ten to get to seventy then nine more for seventy-nine."*

Tests and Quizzes

WHAT ARE THE BENEFITS OF TESTS AND QUIZZES?

Traditional tests and quizzes are often used for assessing skills performance, memorization of facts and definitions, and simple problem solving. Some advantages of tests and quizzes are as follows:

- They are simple and easy to use.

- They give clear results.

- They can be used often.

- They do not require extensive time to grade.

HOW MIGHT TESTS AND QUIZZES BE ALTERED TO MEET OUR ASSESSMENT GOALS?

We may want to consider some changes to make the results of tests and quizzes more useful. Below are some ideas:

- Make the problems and questions richer and more thought requiring. See some of the sample problems throughout this book.

- Hold group discussions of these same topics.

- Ask the students to explain their answers to multiple-choice or true-and-false tests.

  - Why did you choose the answer you chose?

  - What was not right about the other answer choices?

  - What else would you like to add to the question or your answer?

(*Note*: Let's not get carried away with asking students to make explanations or do writing for every assignment or test or quiz. Too much can make students dislike both writing and mathematics.)

- Have the students check their own papers and discuss their answers. This is acceptable because simple tests and quizzes should become less important than other assessments and less likely to influence grades.

- Allow the students to create questions or tests. They should begin by identifying and clarifying what is important enough to test—a good learning experience in itself! They may also include sample responses.

- Maintain a balance of procedures, questions about concepts, explanations of work, and showing work.

Portfolios and Collections of Work

WHAT ARE THE BENEFITS OF PORTFOLIOS?

Portfolios and collections of work can range from a simple folder that holds all a student's work for a period of time to a well-defined and carefully selected "showcase" set of work designed for specific assessment purposes. **Figure 2.16** summarizes some of the benefits of portfolios.

FIG. 2.16

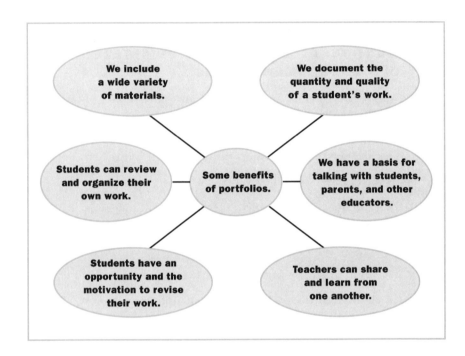

Portfolios and Collections of Work

HOW CAN I HELP STUDENTS BUILD THEIR PORTFOLIOS?

Figure 2.17 is a sample set of guidelines for students (National Center on Education and the Economy and University of Pittsburgh 1997) who are putting together portfolios. Although it may seem wiser to introduce these ideas gradually over time, some teachers who have used portfolios recommend "diving right in" from the beginning of the year. It will be difficult, but if we proceed systematically, the payoff will be worth the work.

FIG. 2.17

Your Mathematics Portfolio

Your mathematics portfolio helps you to show what you have learned in math. We will use it all year long. Here's what goes into it:

1. Papers that show what **math you learned**. Explain what you learned. It's a good idea to have some work from the beginning and some from later on in the year.

2. **Tasks that were really new and hard** for you or that helped you learn a new way of doing math. Explain why the tasks were hard and what you gained.

3. Some **work you did with a group**. Explain how you worked together. What steps did you take? How did you divide up the work?

4. **Ideas from your journal** that tell your attitude toward math.

5. **Include work** that shows that you—

- estimate and predict;
- explore and look for patterns;
- keep working until you are satisfied it's your best work;
- are thorough and careful;
- are well organized;
- look for more than one way to solve a problem;
- are curious and willing to use new ideas.

6. Be sure you show how well you can **communicate about mathematics**.

Organizing:

- **Date:** Be sure to date every paper that goes into your portfolio.
- **Contents:** Make a table of contents or a list of what is in the portfolio.
- **Tasks:** Include the tasks and assignments themselves, so people will understand what you did.
- **Reasons:** Either on the list or on the work, tell why you included each piece. You might want to have a cover sheet for each task.
- **Revisions:** When you review your work, you may want to revise it. Be sure to attach the original to show what you changed and how you improved.
- **Organization:** You are responsible for organizing the work in the portfolio.
- **Help:** If you need help and advice, be sure to ask your teacher.

Portfolios and Collections of Work

The New Standards Project has developed an extensive set of materials to assist teachers in using portfolios as a primary tool in their mathematics assessment program. **Figures 2.18–2.20** show examples of these support materials (National Center on Education and the Economy and University of Pittsburgh 1997).

Figure 2.18, an annotated sample of students' work, illustrates how portfolio entries might be assessed.

FIG. 2.18

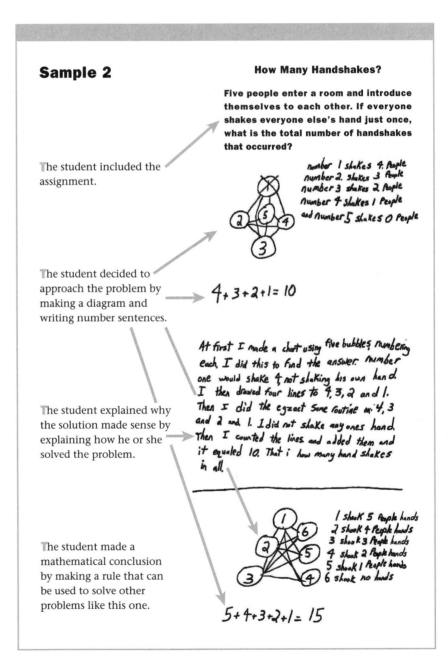

CHAPTER *2*

From *New Standards Performance Standards* (National Center on Education and the Economy and University of Pittsburgh 1997, p. 31). Reprinted with permission.

FIG. 2.18 (Continued)

Sample 2

I noticed a pattern. Since you don't have 6 shake any hands, you write 5, then add 4. then 3 then 2 then 1. and then it equals 15. That pattern helps me to realize not to use a chart on 7 because I can use my way like I did on the pattern. If there where 7 people I would just have to make a math sentence like this:

$$6+5+4+3+2+1=21$$

A way you can always figure it out, without a chart, is by using a math sentence starting at the highest of your number, or the lowest, going up or down then adding all of them together. Remember not to include the person who can't shake his own hand. For exsample if you had 30 people. You might start with 29 because 30 cannot shake his own hand. Then you would count down to 1. Then add all the numbers together and that would equal the correct answer.

The student included the assignment.

The student decided to approach the problem by making a diagram and writing number sentences.

The student explained why the solution made sense by explaining how he or she solved the problem.

The student made a mathematical conclusion by making a rule that can be used to solve other problems like this one.

From *New Standards Performance Standards* (National Center on Education and the Economy and University of Pittsburgh 1997, p. 32). Reprinted with permission.

Portfolios and Collections of Work

READ ABOUT...

■ *Read about an elementary school teacher trying to incorporate a state-mandated portfolio system into her classroom assessment in "Primary Portfolios" in* Mathematics Assessment: Cases and Discussion Questions for Grades K–5, *edited by William S. Bush (2001).*

■ *Read about managing portfolios in "Planning for Classroom Portfolio Assessment" by Diana V. Lambdin and Vicki L. Walker (1994).*

Figure 2.19 shows a self-assessment form for the problem-solving entries that students may have placed in their portfolios.

FIG. 2.19

Problem-Solving Exhibit Instructions

Work That Shows My Problem Solving and Reasoning

_____ I have put four problems in this folder.

This exhibit is complete because—

_____ I included the assignment for each problem (either the copy my teacher gave me or in my own words).

_____ I made important decisions like choosing which diagrams to use, which numbers to use, which strategies to use, etc. (At least three of my four problems show this.)

_____ My solutions make sense and I explained why they make sense. (At least three of my four problems show this.)

_____ I moved beyond the problem (in at least two of my four problems) by doing one of the following:

■ I showed how my solution can be used to help solve a similar problem.

■ I showed how problems like this can help me solve real problems outside school.

■ I showed a pattern or a general rule.

In the problems I put in this folder, I have covered ideas from arithmetic, geometry, measurement, functions, algebra, statistics, and probability. In this folder I don't have to cover all of these ideas.

From *New Standards Performance Standards* (National Center on Education and the Economy and University of Pittsburgh 1997, p. 5). Reprinted with permission.

CHAPTER *2*

Portfolios and Collections of Work

Finally, **figure** 2.20 shows an example of a checklist that students might use to determine whether their portfolio is complete.

FIG. 2.20

Mathematical Concepts
Exhibit Instructions

Table of Contents for the Mathematical Concepts Exhibit

Write the title of each piece of work.

1. Arithmetic and Number _Assembly Chairs_
2. Geometry and Measurement _Square Quilt_
3. Function and Algebra _Square Numbers_
4. Statistics and Probability _Peanut Data (attached)_

Skills and Communication

Use these lists to check all of the work in your exhibit. Make sure your work is correct and clear. Use these lists to help you.

Skills

✓ My arithmetic is correct.

✓ My measurements are correct.

✓ I have used mathematical terms and symbols correctly.

Communication

✓ My work is well organized and detailed.

✓ My work has mathematical vocabulary that I understand.

✓ My work has mathematical representations. I used more than just words and numbers to explain my ideas. I used representations such as diagrams, graphs, and charts.

*Ask your teacher for more information about these categories.

Work That Shows My Understanding of Mathematical Concepts

✓ I have put four pieces of work in this folder. I have included one piece of work from each of these categories:*

Arithmetic and Number, such as—	Geometry and Measurement, such as—
▪ add, subtract, multiply, and divide ▪ use place value ▪ use simple fractions and decimals	▪ work with shapes ▪ use symmetry and congruence ▪ measure length, perimeter, and area
Function and Algebra, such as—	**Statistics and Probability,** such as—
▪ work with linear patterns ▪ work with nonlinear patterns ▪ show what equals (=) means ▪ use variables in simple situations	▪ work with data ▪ use samples ▪ predict and find out what is likely

Each piece of work is complete because—

✓ I included the assignment (either the copy my teacher gave me or in my own words).

✓ I showed how I used the concept to solve problems or do activities.

✓ I used diagrams, charts, graphs, drawings, or words to show I understand the concept. I showed my ideas in more than one way.

✓ I explained what the concept means. For example, "multiplication means ..."

From *New Standards Performance Standards* (National Center on Education and the Economy and University of Pittsburgh 1997, pp. 9–10). Reprinted with permission.

These New Standards materials and much more are listed in the resource list and can be obtained from the National Center on Education and the Economy.

Technology and Assessment

HOW CAN TECHNOLOGY ENHANCE MY CLASSROOM ASSESSMENT PROGRAM?

Although the use of technology in classrooms is a given in many schools, its use for assessment may not be quite so clearly developed. If technological tools are used in learning and instruction, they should also be used during assessment. Technology can serve several purposes in assessment:

■ To help maintain and to assess basic skills

■ To promote mathematics learning

■ To maintain records

■ To further equity and motivation for mathematics students

Basic Skills

Technology does not eliminate the need for students to learn basic mathematics skills—we still need to be able to do addition, subtraction, multiplication, and division with whole numbers, decimals, fractions, and percents without a calculator or computer. Below are some points to consider in relating technology to basic skills assessment.

Promoting and Assessing Mathematics Learning

Technology can promote conceptual understanding and quantitative reasoning when used for solving problems, testing conjectures, and accessing and organizing data. At the elementary level, this happens most often in learning-games programs, although some simulation programs can be used with young students. A big benefit of technology is the practice it affords in using logical steps that can help clarify the way we think. See "Tips from Teachers" below for some suggestions for devloping and assessing the understanding of concepts.

Technology and Assessment

Maintaining Records

Record keeping has probably been the easiest entry into computer use for teachers. Putting test scores and grades into a simple gradebook program can make life much simpler. Look for those that match your curriculum or mathematics textbook.

Equity and Motivation

The analysis of the 1996 National Assessment of Educational Progress results showed that students at the fourth-grade level whose teachers used computers for math-learning games had higher scores than students whose teachers did not. This finding was not true for use of computers primarily for drill. The same report shows that Title I students and African American students are less likely to have teachers who use computers for math-learning games.

With regard to calculators or computers used for drill, we should look for a balance of some assessment that does and some that does not use technological tools. It is important that students develop a facility in using calculators, for instance, as calculators become more complex. Students who do not have that experience, both in daily learning and in testing situations, will be handicapped.

It is also worthwhile to consider the motivational impact of using technology. Many teachers report increased interest and focus on mathematics when technological tools are introduced. Use your imagination and that of your students. For example, have the students make videotapes of their own ideas, such as "The Color Patterns of Numbers" or "How to Use Percents While Shopping." Mathematics can and should be beautiful and exciting!

TIPS FROM TEACHERS

■ *Have the students print out their own progress charts.*

■ *Incorporate printouts into students' reports and record folders.*

■ *Use computers to help with portfolio management (but watch to be sure the computer is simplifying rather than complicating).*

■ *Send home computer-generated reports on students' learning so that parents will be aware of computer use as well as students' learning.*

READ ABOUT...

■ *Read about using technology in assessment in "The Link to Higher Scores," by Jeff Archer (1998).*

Chapter 3

Implementing and Managing Assessment in the Classroom: How Do I Use the Tools?

Teacher-to-Teacher

I've found some assessment tasks that look pretty good—at least they're different from those we've used in the past. They seem to be asking students to think a little more. But I have lots more questions. How can I be sure that I'm using the right kinds of assessments? How do I record what I see students doing or what I see in their work? How can all of us at my school make our standards and expectations clear? What about student self-assessment? Accountability? How do I help all students with assessment?

READ ABOUT...

■ **Read about** developing assessment plans in Mathematics Assessment: Myths, Models, Good Questions, and Practical Suggestions, *edited by Jean K. Stenmark (1991).*

■ **Read about** an elementary school teacher's struggle to plan balanced assessment in "How Do I Assess Thee? Let Me Count the Ways..." in Mathematics Assessment: Cases and Discussion Questions for Grades K–5, *edited by William S. Bush (2001).*

■ **Read about** planning assessment in "The Process of Assessment Applied to Tessellations," by Janet Sharp and Karen Bush Hoiberg (1998).

Making Assessment Plans

Some of our assessment will be prescribed by factors outside the classroom. We may be required to use the chapter tests that come with a textbook series, or we may have to anticipate standardized testing at some time during the year. Our primary responsibility in those instances is to be aware of what is covered in the tests and to give students as much preparation as is practical. If long division is on the test, students should encounter some long division during instruction. If they will have to write explanations or draw diagrams, those skills should be practiced. In the classroom, however, we can use assessments that directly help us understand what students know and what we can do in order to help them do better work.

HOW DO I PLAN FOR ASSESSMENT IN MY CLASSROOM?

In developing a plan for assessment, it is important for us to work with others, either in a grade-level group or as a whole school. A colleague across the hall can be a great help in making decisions about how we assess our students' work. As we plan, some of the questions we may want to discuss include the following:

■ *Material to be covered.* What in our curriculum is worth assessing? What is the most important mathematics? What can we find out about students' learning?

■ *Standards.* What specific mathematics and quality of work are we looking for? What do we expect of students?

■ *Criteria.* What is important to assess? For example, is a correct answer without an explanation as good as one that has a slight error but a good explanation? Will we consider writing skills such as spelling in the scoring?

■ *Types of assessment.* What assessments do we want to use? How do they fit together? Which kinds of assessment will work best for our classrooms? Discuss—

■ tests;

■ open-ended questions;

■ performance tasks, investigations, and so on;

■ observations, interviews, questions, and conferences;

■ portfolios for individual students;

■ portfolios of the work of the entire class;

■ the effect of tests from outside the classroom.

- *Scheduling.* Assessment is constant in the classroom; how often do we want to document what we see or hear?

- *Time.* How can we best use our time for assessment? What plan can we make for consulting with one another to find assessment material, look at student work, and continue the program?

- *Preparation.* What materials will we need? Should we have copies made, or collect pencils, blocks, calculators, and so on?

- *Support.* What part do school administrators play in the process? What part will students play in the process?

Clearly, planning assessment is not a project that can be completed in a couple of short faculty meetings. It takes time to make all these decisions. It also takes time to keep the assessment a living documentation of progress by performing an ongoing review of what we have done, what we may need to change, and what we can do next. To make the task easier we can—

- work and talk with other teachers to keep ourselves sane and on track;

- try one thing at a time;

- draw on materials already available, such as those listed in the bibliography;

- look through the rest of this book for ideas.

Above all, developing a sensible assessment system or program will involve—

- making sure that students participate from start to finish;

- using assessment tools and topics that fit what we do in class every day;

- keeping all the necessary people—students, other teachers, school staff such as counselors and administrators, and parents—involved.

Chapter Overview

In this chapter you will learn about—

- **making assessment plans;**

- **documenting observations;**

- **checklists;**

- **feedback to students;**

- **student involvement and self-assessment;**

- **managing portfolios;**

- **helping students write in mathematics;**

- **equity and special needs;**

- **assessment beyond the classroom;**

- **managing time and logistics.**

TIPS FROM TEACHERS

A process for planning might be to take one especially important topic for a grade level and follow these steps:

- *Identify three to five important concepts.*

- *Identify two activities that use each of the important concepts.*

- *Decide on preliminary criteria that can indicate whether students have succeeded in learning the concepts.*

- *Find or write three kinds of assessment that we want to use, perhaps one true-false test, one short-answer test, and one weeklong project or task.*

- *Set a date for having these assessments ready for students' use.*

- *Think about needed revisions as we watch students work.*

- *Set a date to meet and look at students' work.*

- *Revise activities, assessment tasks, and criteria as needed.*

Documenting Observations

Documentation is a vital part of assessment. We are used to keeping track of numbers and grades in our gradebooks, but now a more useful record is required. When we give added importance to observations, interviews, and group work, most of us need to develop the habit of putting on paper the reasons for our conclusions. In an age of accountability, we have to be able to explain our decisions.

WHY IS GOOD DOCUMENTATION OF OBSERVATIONS IMPORTANT?

By doing ongoing, nonstructured observations, we assess students in context. Students will show their learning in authentic ways. In order to capture students' learning, we must use different documentation strategies. This documentation serves a variety of purposes:

- It helps us remember what we have seen and heard.
- It guides our instruction.
- It reveals patterns of learning or behavior over time.
- It provides evidence of learning.
- It supports discussions with parents or other teachers.

WHAT DOCUMENTATION METHODS CAN I USE FOR OBSERVATIONS?

Documentation methods range from informal to formal. Jottings and anecdotal notes are useful for daily classroom observations, but narratives and running records are more likely to serve the purpose if a special focus is desired or if a particular question is to be considered. Narratives and running records may require another adult—an aide, parent, or counselor—in the room to monitor the class while the teacher records his or her observations. The details of narratives or running records may become overwhelming if we try to do this for many students or many activities.

CHAPTER *3*

Documenting Observations

Some common methods of documentation are as follows:

Jottings

- Brief notes
- Written while interacting with students
- Reminders of what has been observed
- Details may be added later.
- Notes may be written about more than one student during an observation.

Anecdotal Notes

- More detailed than jottings
- May be written while interacting with students
- Describe a particular event
- Details may be added later.
- Notes may be written about more than one student during an observation.

Narratives

- More detailed than anecdotal notes
- Usually written when observer is not interacting with a student
- Everything that is said and done by a student is recorded as it happens.
- Includes information about student-to-student interactions
- May include multiple instructional objectives

Running Records

- Similar to narratives
- Focus on one instructional objective
- Usually written when observer is not interacting with a student
- Written about only one student at a time
- Everything that is said and done by a student related to the focus objective is recorded as it happens.

Documenting Observations

EXAMPLES OF DOCUMENTATION

Jenny's third-grade class has done some work with multiplication and is ready to begin using what they have learned in real-life situations. They are used to "pretend buying" activities and are comfortable with using calculators and price sheets. A possible use of multiplication is built into this activity by asking students to buy three ice-cream cones. Jenny does not tell her students to use multiplication, nor does she give any directions for solving the problem other than what is printed on the sheet distributed to the class. Students work independently, although ideas may be shared. Jenny circulates around the room, documents information, and interacts with students. The task that they worked on is in **figure 3.1**.

FIG. 3.1

You and two friends spent the afternoon at Casey's Carnival. Your mother gives you $20 to spend on food for all of you. You know that each of you will buy an ice-cream cone before leaving.

1. Show what you will buy to eat. Remember to include both the name of each food and its price.

2. Show the total amount you will pay and the change you will receive.

3. Show that you have enough money to buy 3 ice-cream cones.

Casey's Carnival Snack Menu

Hot dogs	89¢	Pretzels	59¢/bag
Pizza		French Fries	$1.65
Cheese	$1.00/slice	Cheese	25¢ extra
Pepperoni	$1.35/slice		
Nachos	$3.29	Potato Chips	69¢/bag
Peppers	25¢ extra		
Soda Pop		Ice-Cream Cones	99¢
Small	75¢		
Medium	$1.00		
Large	$1.25	All prices include tax.	

CHAPTER *3*

Documenting Observations

Figures 3.2–3.5 are examples of four students' work on the Casey's Carnival problem; an example of jottings is given for each figure, and an example of a different form of documentation accompanies each figure.

Jottings

Bobbi buys the ice cream first so that she doesn't forget it.

Dolores uses the calculator to do repeated addition for the multiple items purchased.

Bruce buys the food first and gives a total. He then shows that he has enough to buy 3 ice-cream cones.

Dantae includes the number of items, price per unit, and subtotal for each item. He uses multiplication.

Anecdotal Notes

Bobbi

Says the three kids will each eat a hot dog, an ice-cream cone, and a soda and share the french fries and the pretzels. She remembers the addition sign and the subtraction sign. She uses the calculator to add the column of prices but does the subtraction herself (trades across zeros). Checks her answer using the calculator.

(or notes may be in a list format)

Dolores

- *The kids should all eat the same food.*

- *Writes the 3 before the ice-cream cones because "that's what the problem said."*

- *Doesn't use dollar signs but can rewrite the cent value as a dollar value.*

- *Uses the calculator for all parts and correctly adds and subtracts.*

- *Uses repeated addition for the prices.*

- *Doesn't represent the problems on the page of work.*

- *Answers are correct.*

FIG. 3.2

Bobbi   Casey's Carnival

Food   Price
iCe Cream   99¢
Ice Cream   99¢
ice cream   99¢
French Fries $1.65
hot dog   89¢
hot dog   89¢
hot dog   89¢
Pretzels   59¢
Small Soda   75¢
Small Soda   75¢
Small Soda   +75¢

total $10.13

$20.00
-$10.13
$ 9.87 change

FIG. 3.3

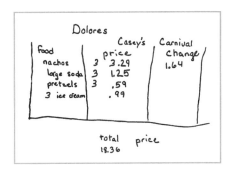

Dolores
                    Casey's Carnival
Food   price   change
nachos   3   3.29   1.64
large soda 3 1.25
pretzels   3   .59
3 ice cream   .99

total   price
18.36

Documenting Observations

FIG. 3.4

Narratives and Running Records

(Useful for focusing on one student or one difficulty)

Bruce decides that each kid will eat only one item, but all will need something to drink. He constructs two columns and lists the item in one and the price in the other. The total price of the three drinks is calculated using mental math: "1 + 1 + 1 is 3 and 25 + 25 + 25 is 75." He correctly places both dollar signs and cent signs. He adds the prices using the calculator. He is able to independently enter the cents as ".89." He uses the calculator to figure the change, entering "20.00 – 8.93 =," and correctly records the answer. He rereads the directions and figures the total price of three ice-cream cones using repeated addition. He records the price and the change using the change received from the first purchase. He then decides to write the explanation of the purchase as a word problem.

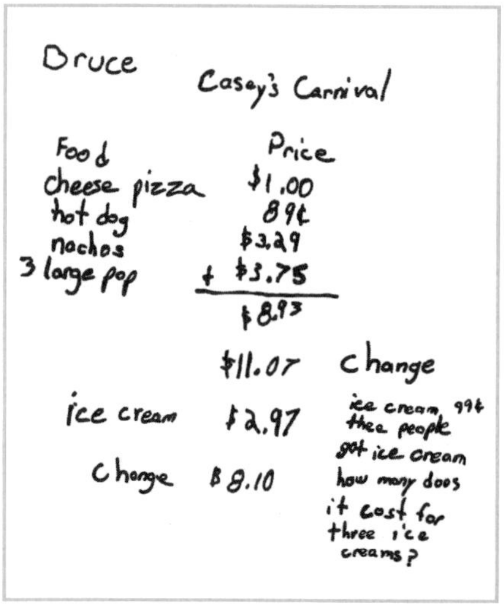

Multiplication Focus

Dantae constructs a food column and a price column. He decides that each kid will have the same food and includes the ice cream in the list. He records the price per unit, then records the subtotal for the items. He enters each problem on the calculator as "3 unit price =." He records the subtotal with a dollar sign and a decimal point.

FIG. 3.5

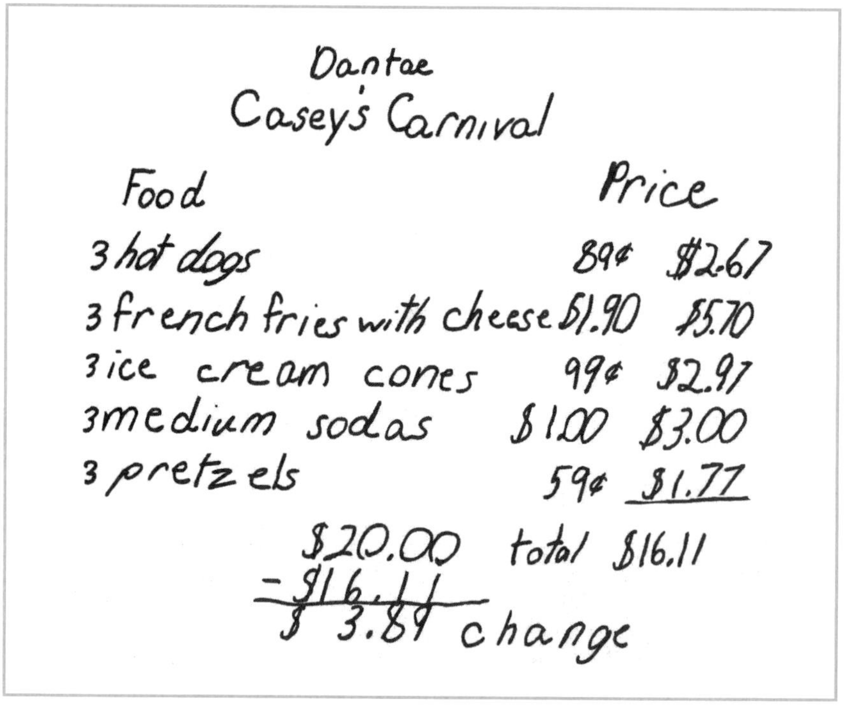

Documenting Observations

WHAT TOOLS CAN I USE TO DOCUMENT OBSERVATIONS?

Before an observation or other assessment begins, choose an appropriate method and tool for documenting the assessment, depending on the focus and type of observation. When making a choice, consider the following:

- *Focus of the observation.* What information do I want to get?

- *Students involved.* Which students am I observing?

- *Observer's preference.* What method or tool do I feel most comfortable using?

- *Time.* How long will the observation last?

- *Need for details.* Do I need detailed information?

- *Use of results.* How will this information be used?

With practice, we can develop the documentation methods best suited to our styles. Some of the tools teachers have used to document students' progress are listed below. With time and practice, we may find it easier to decide which tool to use for different situations.

Self-Stick Notes

Various sizes of self-stick notes can hold jottings and anecdotal comments. Be sure to include the student's name on each one. Notes can be filed in a notebook or folder at the end of the day.

Mailing Labels or Computer Labels

Use these as you would self-stick notes, but leave the labels on the original sheet until the end of the day, so they aren't so likely to get lost or stuck on other papers. If you have access to a computer and a printer, names can be printed on the labels, making it easy to know which children you plan to observe.

Index Cards

Write each student's name on an index card for observation notes. Since you will use more than one card for each student, number the cards in order. Keep the cards on a clipboard or on a ring. File them in a box or in individual folders.

Documenting Observations

Class Checklists

Make multiple copies of a list of students with a check-off grid. For any particular observation, various skills, objectives, or behaviors may be listed across the top. Make a check for each student who exhibits the appropriate behavior. Keep the checklists in a notebook or on a clipboard.

Monthly Calendars

Take a monthly calendar and write one student's name on each school day. Record observations on the calendar. After the month has ended, cut the calendar apart and file notes in individual student folders. This method ensures that one student will be observed each day.

Notebooks

Notebooks can be used in various ways. In a loose-leaf notebook, with a divider for each student, you can store notes of several kinds, as well as grids and other forms. Spiral notebooks work well for jottings during a class observation with a single focus. Cut all but the last left-hand page on the left margin line. List students' names down the right margin of the last right-hand page. At the top of each page list the date and the focus of the observation. Write your jottings on the line beside each student's name.

Electronic Recording Devices

Tape recorders and video cameras can record students' activity, too. Recordings may be played at a later date for a more intensive review and documentation. Recorded observation notes may be transcribed at a later time. (*Note*: Before making videotapes of students, check with your local administration for legality and the need for parent permission.)

Computers

As more computers become available for teachers' use, the possibilities for documentation increase. Word-processing or database programs should be explored for easy recording. These programs can make the transmission of information to next year's teacher easy, too.

CHAPTER *3*

Checklists

HOW CAN CHECKLISTS BE USED?

We've already talked about recording information from observations and conversations. Sometimes we may not want to, or not have time to, record observations. We may want more structure. For example, oral reports may be evaluated without keeping records, and students' peers can take part as a way of understanding what they need to do for their own presentations. **Figure 3.6** shows a short checklist that might be used by a student in preparing for a presentation and by both students and teachers in evaluating presentations.

FIG. 3.6

READ ABOUT...

■ *Read about checklists in "Activating Assessment Alternatives in Mathematics," by David Clarke (1992).*

Oral Report Check Sheet

Problem solving

_____ The math was clear and well explained.

_____ More than one way of solving the problem was used.

_____ The answers were correct and made sense.

_____ All parts of the problem were used or considered.

_____ The work went beyond what the problem required.

Presentation and communication

_____ The visuals were easy to understand.

_____ The presentation was well organized.

_____ The explanations were clear and logical.

_____ The voice was clear.

Suggestions for revision:

Feedback to Students

WHEN DO I PROVIDE FEEDBACK TO STUDENTS?

Feedback for students starts with their understanding the criteria used in the assessment before the assessment happens. They will then already have a pretty good idea of how well they have done on an assessement. Along with feedback from observations, journals, projects, and portfolios, students' experiences with standards, rubrics, and self-assessment will give them far more information than they had in the past. In addition, conferences and interviews give as much information to the student as to the teacher.

HOW DO I PROVIDE FEEDBACK TO STUDENTS?

Feedback can take many different forms. Instead of saying, "This is what you did wrong," or "This is what you need to do," we can ask questions: "What do you think you need to do? What other strategy choices could you make? Have you thought about ...?"

Students can help define standards, create rubrics, plan their own projects, and manage their own portfolios. Doing so helps them understand and value the process of learning. We actively involve students with the assessment system. The more they understand what is going to happen, the more comfortable they will feel. Although elementary school students may not understand the technicalities of standardized testing and letter grades, they do know the anxiety of "test day."

As teachers and adults, we have the responsibility for guidance and direction. It will sometimes be necessary to be direct and tell students what they need to do or what they have failed to do. Especially when we begin to make changes in our assessment practices, some students will feel very insecure and need to depend on adults for information. Introducing these students gradually and slowly to evaluating their own work can provide some magical breakthroughs in understanding. We can ask them and ourselves, "Which is more important, that you get this one problem right or that you learn to judge for yourself whether this is your best work?"

Feedback to Students

Figure 3.7 presents a list of questions that students or teachers can consider about how students approach work done in class. Such a list could become an evaluation form or a wall chart.

FIG. 3.7

1. How do I get started with my work?

- Ask another student.
- Ask the teacher.
- Self-start.

2. What do I do to get "unstuck"?

- Ask another student.
- Ask the teacher.
- Ask my group for ideas.
- Look up more information.

3. How do I ask for help?

- Where do I begin?
- I don't understand any of it.
- Can you explain this part to me?
- What do I do next?

4. I've checked the words that apply to me.

___ Show initiative ___ Stick to it ___ Am on task ___ Do more that I have to

TIPS FROM TEACHERS

■ *Instead of teacher comments in journals, on problem solutions, reports, and other work, pose written questions that lead to more thinking.*

■ *Attach blank rating sheets to assignments and have students fill them out.*

■ *Use checklists for activities and classroom work.*

READ ABOUT...

Read about a teacher's concerns about providing feedback to students as they tackle an open-ended task in "Open Car Wash" in Mathematics Assessment: Cases and Discussion Questions for Grades 6–12, *edited by William S. Bush (2000).*

Explain and model the role students play in assessment. Students will be responsible not only for the work itself but for reflections, explanations, interviews, and conferences. Before the year begins, mail students a letter explaining the changes they will see. Be positive about the year, and ask them for help. The first day should then be filled with excited anticipation about assessment changes.

Student Involvement and Self-Assessment

WHY IS STUDENT SELF-ASSESSMENT IMPORTANT?

Student self-assessment can become one of our most important goals. By self-assessment we do not mean that students simply grade their own papers or tell us what their grades should be. We want all students to become independent learners, able to look critically at their own work. Without understanding the quality of their work, students cannot improve it. A student should be able to ask herself or himself, "Is this the best work I can do on this problem, or is there more I need to think about? Have I given a complete explanation? Am I sure it is all correct? Could I find another way of working on it? Is there another answer?"

Not all feedback has to come from outside—it can come from within. When adults assume that they must be the ones who tell students whether their work is good enough, they leave them handicapped, not only in testing situations (such as standardized tests) in which they must perform without guidance but in life itself. Who is a better employee, one who always waits to be told what to do and whether it is good enough or one who can evaluate the quality of his or her own work and change as needed?

HOW CAN I GET MY STUDENTS MORE INVOLVED IN ASSESSMENT?

For students to be appropriately engaged in self-assessment, the standards and assessments must be open. That is, students need to—

- be aware of what is valued and what is important;

- discuss what makes work good or not so good;

- participate in defining standards and criteria;

- see examples of both good and poor work;

- understand such assessment techniques as rubrics;

- study for purposes that they understand and accept;

- be encouraged to reflect on and analyze their own work.

CHAPTER *3*

Student Involvement and Self-Assessment

Some experiences that will help students develop the habit of self-assessment include—

- selecting and organizing their own work for portfolios, revising their selections as needed, and identifying what needs to be added;

- discussing standards and criteria in groups or whole-class meetings;

- regularly writing comments to the teacher, in journals or on work papers;

- asking and answering questions during class discussions or presentations;

- learning to ask pertinent questions of one another;

- responding to self-evaluation checklists;

- scoring sample sets of student papers according to rubrics;

- creating rubrics for new problems or tasks;

- having continued opportunities to revise drafts to produce the best work they can;

- realizing that they can sometimes learn more from mistakes than from getting everything right.

Developing self-assessment is a long-term process. We can begin to foster it as soon as children come to school. It requires lots of discussing and rediscussing. Feedback from adults helps children form ideas about what good work looks like, but teachers' leading questions are sometimes better than directive or corrective feedback and help students understand that they can control their own success.

Student Involvement and Self-Assessment

Figures 3.8, **3.9**, and **3.10** are sample self-assessment forms. Begin the year by having students focus on one question at a time. For example, the questions in **figure 3.8** might be a topic for group discussions or serve as individual journal prompts for two weeks. The same questions might also be used near the end of the year.

FIG. 3.8

Reflective questions

Name _____

Date _____

Please answer the following questions using complete sentences. Be thoughtful. Be truthful. Use you best handwriting and spelling.

Which math skills are you good at now?

Which math skills would you like to be better at?

What could you do to improve your math?

Student Involvement and Self-Assessment

Self-evaluation sheets can also be tailored to a particular problem:

Today is the thirty-fifth day of school. As we have done before, use the space below to record as many ways as you can of representing the number 35. Then turn the sheet over and complete the sentences.

The problem and space to work are on the front of the sheet, and the self-evaluation form (**fig. 3.9**) is on the back.

FIG. 3.9

Name _____

Date _____

The assignment was to _____

_____

_____

A new way I represented this number was _____

_____

_____

By doing this problem I have learned that _____

_____

_____

The hardest thing about this problem was _____

_____

_____

The next time we do a problem like this, I would like to try _____

_____

_____

Student Involvement and Self-Assessment

READ ABOUT...

■ *Read about a fourth-grade teacher who involves her students in assessment in "Students as Assessors" in* Mathematics Assessment: Cases and Discussion Questions for Grades K–5, *edited by William S. Bush (2001).*

■ *Read about students assessing group work in "A Teacher's View on Classroom Assessment: What and How?" by De A. Tonack (1996).*

■ *Read about student self-assessment in "The STEM Model," by Rick Billstein (1998).*

The example in **figure 3.10** is written to be used by a group, but it (or one of your own devising) could certainly be used with individual students. The questions (and others) could be made into a poster for classroom reference. A list can also communicate goals and methods to parents. And, of course, the questions should be changed to fit your own students' needs.

FIG. 3.10

Name(s) _____ Date _____

Good, Better, Best Work

How did we check our answers?_____

_____

_____

Did we find more than one way to solve the problem or more than one answer?

Explain._____

_____

Did our diagram help us solve the problem? Explain. _____

_____

_____

How can we do more than the problem asks for?_____

_____

_____

What did we learn from doing this problem? _____

_____

_____

Did we work well together?_____

_____

_____

CHAPTER *3*

Managing Portfolios

WHAT FORM MAY PORTFOLIOS TAKE?

Although a collection of students' work may be the beginning of a portfolio, a portfolio is more than that. Portfolios include selected pieces of work that illustrate both the mathematics and the quality of thinking that students and the teacher want to highlight. A working portfolio, usually a manila folder, can be temporary storage. A permanent portfolio (a colored folder or a folder with a colored label) will be the collection spot for identified selections that have been processed according to predetermined guidelines.

HOW CAN I INCORPORATE PORTFOLIOS INTO MY CLASSROOM ASSESSMENT?

Here are some helpful hints to make portfolios work:

- Keep portfolios accessible as working tools. Use tubs or boxes kept on shelves.

- Post guidelines and examples near the permanent portfolio shelf. Students (and parents) might also have their own copies of the guidelines.

- Have whole-class discussions about the examples and guidelines to clarify them and to be sure that students understand.

- Try peer evaluation of portfolios with the guidance of the teacher.

The student guidelines might include requirements such as these:

- Name and dates

- Table of contents

- The titles of the assignments or copies of them

- Cover sheets with information to clarify what the work is about

- Reflections about the work students included and what they were thinking

Chapter 2 also includes examples of student guidelines for portfolios.

Managing Portfolios

Figures **3.11**, **3.12**, and **3.13** are descriptions of a complete portfolio, types of entries, and portfolio "thinking questions" for reflection that were offered by Diana V. Lambdin and Vicki L. Walker (1994) in an article on managing portfolios in the *Arithmetic Teacher*.

FIG. 3.11

Mathematics Portfolio Entries

A complete portfolio will include—

- a completed table of contents;

- a letter to the reviewer written by the student that describes the portfolio;

- five best entries reflective of the topics studied and the activities completed in the course.

Each entry must include the original question, task, or problem posed; a title; the date; and the student's name. Entries must be in the same order as listed in the Table of Contents and must be numbered accordingly. If an entry is in the category of photographs, audiotapes, videotapes, or computer disks, then the entry must be accompanied by a brief paragraph describing the activity and its rationale.

(Adapted from Kentucky Department of Education [1992, 1–4])

From Lambdin and Walker (1994, p. 320)

Managing Portfolios

FIG. 3.12

Mathematics Portfolio Entry Types

Writing

This type of entry includes journal entries, mathematics autobiographies, explanations, reflections, justifications, and so on.

Investigations or Discovery

This type of entry can be described as an exploration that leads to understanding of mathematical ideas or to the formulation of mathematical generalizations. Examples include gathering data, examining models, constructing arguments, and performing simulations.

Application

This type of entry is to include the selection and use of concepts, principles, and procedures to solve problems in a well-grounded, real-world context.

Interdisciplinary

This type of entry demonstrates the use of mathematics within other disciplines.

Nonroutine Problems

This type of entry includes problems for which the solution or strategies are not immediately evident. This category may include mathematical recreations such as puzzles and logic problems.

Projects

This type of entry includes activities that extend over a period of days and requires a formal presentation of the material learned. This category may include research projects, designs, constructions, and original computer programs.

Note: A portfolio entry may fall into more than one of the foregoing types.

(Adapted from Kentucky Department of Education [1992, 1–4])

From Lambdin and Walker (1994, p. 320)

Managing Portfolios

FIG. 3.13

Portfolio "Thinking Questions"

Please think through these questions carefully as you begin finalizing your portfolio selections and preparing your written summaries.

- What activity or mathematical topic was involved?

- How did the activity help you learn something new?

- What did you learn from this experience?

- Can you describe any connections between the activity and other subject areas or real-life situations?

- Would you do anything differently if you had more time?

- What strategies did you use? (What did you *think* as you worked through the task?)

- What mathematical skills were used in your solution process?

- How would you rate your overall performance related to the activity?

- What are your areas of strength in mathematics?

- What goals have you set for yourself in mathematics?

From Lambdin and Walker (1994, p. 321)

Managing Portfolios

HOW DO I GRADE OR EVALUATE PORTFOLIOS?

Grading or evaluating portfolios does take time. First, it's necessary to decide on criteria. Some states or districts have instituted portfolio programs, and in those cases the criteria are already decided and teachers can use them in their classrooms. Some of the evaluation categories other teachers might want to consider are—

- mathematical content;
- the use of mathematics skills and processes;
- communication;
- thinking;
- tools and techniques;
- attitudes toward mathematics;
- the diversity of selections;
- whether explanations or reflections are included;
- organization;
- evidence of change over time.

Be selective in choosing categories. Too many will make the task too difficult for both student and teacher. Some teachers prefer to score individual selections of a portfolio and total these scores for a portfolio score. Others prefer to give a general score to the whole portfolio. (See holistic and analytic rubrics in chapter 4 for a discussion of the advantages of each preference.)

One strategy for evaluating portfolios might be to sort them into three stacks that represent "excellent," "satisfactory," and "needs improvement." The teacher can then go back and do a more thorough reading, possibly a separate reading for each category that will be assessed. Some teachers find that a thorough reading and scoring the first time through is more efficient. Try both ways to choose the one that works best for you.

Managing Portfolios

READ ABOUT...

■ *Read about a teacher's use of state-mandated portfolios in "Primary Portfolio" in* Mathematics Assessment: Cases and Discussion Questions for Grades K–5, *edited by William S. Bush (2001).*

■ *Read about planning portfolio assessment in "Planning for Classroom Portfolio Assessment," by Diana V. Lambdin and Vicki L. Walker (1994).*

WHAT DO I DO WITH COMPLETED AND SCORED PORTFOLIOS?

At the end of the year, students are ready to go on, but what happens to a scored portfolio? Some districts or individual schools have policies about their disposition, but in others, teachers may have to make the decisions. Teachers in a school or district should try to establish a consistent policy for the school or district. An important consideration always to keep in mind is that the portfolio work belongs to the students. That is not to say that the work cannot be kept. Here are some options:

■ *Send everything home.* If evidence of the student's progress exists otherwise and is a part of the permanent record, the portfolio might be sent home in its entirety at the end of the year. (You might want to suggest to parents that this is a good record of growth and that they may want to keep it.)

■ *Keep some, send some home.* This is the most popular option, since the portfolio reveals more about a student than a letter grade or a standardized test ever could. How much to keep and how much to send home is the dilemma. Some teachers decide which pieces best show progress at different times in the year. These entries go into the student's file and the rest goes home. Sometimes the students and the teacher make the decision together. The students include reflections about their learning and other information they think next year's teacher should know. Again, the rest is sent home. Another decision must be made in the fall after the receiving teacher has reviewed the work. Some schools send the "mini" portfolio home in October after they have reviewed it. Others select a few pieces to be kept in the permanent record until the student is promoted to middle school, and the rest is sent home. With the "keep some, send some home" option, the portfolio is reviewed and cleaned out regularly. With any of the options listed here, input should be sought from the students, teachers, administrators, and parents before a decision is made.

■ *Keep it all.* If the portfolio is the only evidence to show the student's progress, then it must become part of the permanent record. However, storage space for all portfolios of all students for just elementary school has posed problems for some schools. If so, considering one of the earlier options may be necessary. If the school has the capability, scanning the work and creating a portfolio computer disk for each student may be feasible.

In any of these options, care must be taken to include the pertinent documentation. Anyone looking at the work should be able to find the student's name, the assignment, and the date completed. Additional notes may reflect the student's approach to the assignment as well as the completeness and accuracy of the student's work.

CHAPTER **3**

Helping Students Write in Mathematics

One issue that arises with changes in assessment is the difficulty some students may have with the amount of writing required. In the past, we have not often expected students to do much writing. Now, however, with increased emphasis on asking students to explain their thinking and the steps they have taken to solve problems, writing in mathematics becomes an important skill.

HOW CAN I IMPROVE MY STUDENTS' WRITING IN MATHEMATICS?

We may need to establish a regular program of instruction in writing within the mathematics class. Here are some ideas.

- *Verbalizing.* Writing begins with verbalizing.

  - Have students work in groups or with partners, explaining to each other what a problem means and restating it in their own words.

  - Suggest that they pretend they are explaining a problem to an alien and that they try to be sure the alien understands.

  - Ask them to tell someone else the rules of a game or the steps for doing a simple task, such as sharpening a pencil.

  - If necessary, allow students to dictate their answers to a parent or adult volunteer, who will write down their exact words.

- *Writing.* Write often, but not to excess.

  - Have students keep a daily log of work on a long task, such as a problem of the week, and then write up the process as a whole.

  - Have students write for a variety of audiences—relatives, friends, famous people, imaginary people or creatures, their own toys, and so on.

  - Ask them to write step-by-step directions for doing a math problem.

  - Allow students to ask for the correct spelling of a word or phrase, which then goes on the chalkboard or onto a vocabulary list.

Helping Students Write in Mathematics

READ ABOUT...

■ *Read about* writing in mathematics class in "The Missing Link? Writing in Mathematics Class," by John Ciochine and Grace Polivka (1997).

■ *Organizing ideas for writing.* Group the ideas.

■ Introduce a simple format. Solve a simple word problem with the whole class participating and the teacher writing the steps on the board or overhead projector.

■ Ask—

■ "What do we know from the problem?" (Make a list.)

■ "What do we need to find out?"

■ "What can we do first? Next?"

■ "What are the results?"

■ Brainstorm with the class or group about a topic, getting as many ideas as possible. Then pick one idea that might make a good beginning. Decide which other suggestions are related, and put them together to go into the first paragraph. Choose another item and its related ideas. Continue grouping like ideas until most of the brainstormed ideas have been used. Ask the students to write an article about the topic, using the groups of ideas.

■ *Revising.* Make the work better.

■ Form groups and have the children share their work with one another, getting suggestions for changes or additions. One way to start is to give students a copy of a short mathematics story the teacher has written and ask for suggestions to make it better.

Equity and Special Needs

Current modes of assessment can offer wonderful opportunities for students to show their learning, but they can also be a terrible trap for students who are not prepared. We have a responsibility to avoid assessment practices that may cause some students to fail.

HOW CAN I BE EQUITABLE IN MY ASSESSMENT PRACTICES?

It is important to let students and parents know that making problems harder or more open is not intended as trickery. It is meant to increase students' chances of success rather than to cause confusion. For example, teachers are accustomed to considering a well-worded problem better than one that is poorly worded. We have looked for explicit directions that will lead to a correct answer. Now teachers look for problems that will help students learn to think, make decisions, and plan their own strategies. We want students to choose to use blocks or diagrams to solve a problem rather than tell them what strategy to use.

Consider the standards for equitable assessments in **figure 3.14** and the related remedies that can help teachers eliminate deficiencies in assessments.

FIG. 3.14

Standard	Remedies
■ The content is such that all students have had an opportunity to learn it.	■ Review the assessment to ensure that it matches the curriculum and daily work.
■ Language—the wording and vocabulary are within the experience of students.	■ Introduce and discuss new words. ■ Have assessments reviewed by people who have special knowledge of students (parents, community members, members of other cultural groups, etc.). ■ Translate the assessment into the student's first language, if needed. ■ Use visual cues, such as illustrative pictures and diagrams.
■ The reading level is appropriate.	■ Reword the problems. ■ Read the problems aloud to students. ■ Make a tape of the problems that students can listen to.
■ The required responses are within students' abilities or skills.	■ Give children many experiences in writing out explanations of their work. ■ Value diagrams, drawings, charts, or other forms of response. ■ Accept oral responses.
■ The context and the required information are familiar to students.	■ Check with other teachers or parents to ensure students' familiarity. ■ Ask students if they know about the contents and context. ■ Provide alternative questions or choices. ■ Incorporate situations from students' daily lives.
■ The tasks or questions make sense to students.	■ Listen when students put the problems into their own words. ■ Discuss the problems with students. ■ Have students discuss the problems in small groups.
■ The standards or criteria are clear to students.	■ Have students help define the standards and criteria. ■ Discuss the standards, criteria, and rubrics. ■ Give students samples of good and not-so-good student work to review and discuss.
■ Problems are accessible to students but offer challenge and "stretching of minds."	■ Begin the year by telling students what is expected, but move later to saying, "You know the kinds of things I have looked for when you worked other problems. Keep those in mind while you work. Let me know how you are solving the problem."

Equity and Special Needs

HOW CAN I ENSURE THAT MY ASSESSMENT IS SENSITIVE TO STUDENTS WITH SPECIAL NEEDS?

With the growing trend toward full inclusion, we are faced with the possibility of a wider range of abilities in our classes. Special-needs students as well as gifted students will be assessed with their peers. Because we provide developmentally appropriate learning and assessment experiences and refer to age- or grade-level objectives, students with special needs have a natural place in our assessment system. Through portfolios and narrative reports, both expectations and performance can be reported with more clarity than a letter grade could ever reveal.

Many established lessons and assessments can be adapted to meet the needs of diverse learners. The chart in **figure 3.15** shows how teachers who are starting the challenging task of meeting the needs of *all* learners can begin to adapt their practices. In **figure 3.16** is an example of a lesson plan that has been adapted to meet the needs of students in special programs. Chapter 5 includes a blackline master for the adapted lesson plan.

FIG. 3.15

I could adapt—	This means I will—	In math, I could—
Time	■ Increase or decrease the time allotted for instruction, completing a task, or assessment.	■ Provide extra time for completing work. ■ Allow students to move through material at their own pace.
Amount	■ Increase or decrease the number of tasks or assessment items the student is expected to complete.	■ Reduce the number of problems. ■ Eliminate practice for the students who know the material already.
Difficulty	■ Adapt the skill level of the task or the assessment tool.	■ Use materials on student's instructional level. ■ Rewrite current curriculum materials to match the student's instructional level.
Instruction	■ Adapt how the student receives instruction.	■ Plan for all learning styles within a lesson or assessment—visual, auditory, kinesthetic, tactile. ■ Plan hands-on activities.
Format	■ Adapt how the student demonstrates knowledge.	■ Arrange for oral rather than written responses. ■ Allow the student to select a presentation format.
Manipulatives	■ Provide additional, varied manipulatives for completing the task or assessment.	■ Encourage students to develop personal strategies for solving problems. ■ Allow students to use calculators.
Support	■ Provide additional, individual support for extending or reteaching objectives.	■ Organize peer buddies or tutors and cross-age buddies for tutors. ■ Provide the student individual time with the teacher or other adults.
Curriculum	■ Substitute objectives on the basis of individual goals.	■ Allow independent research and projects. ■ Adapt the curriculum to meet the goals of the individualized eduction plan.

CHAPTER *3*

Equity and Special Needs

FIG. 3.16

Adapted Lesson Plan

Objective: To review multiplication facts by making up and solving number stories about equal groups of objects

Instructional Plan: Lesson will be introduced with the math message: 5 packages of pencils. 6 pencils per pack. How many pencils? Students will solve & discuss problem as a group. Students will write 2 problems independently and share.

Assessment Plan: Students work will be assessed for accuracy during the lesson.

Name(s) of students(s) needing lesson adaptions:

Tyler   Emily
Amy   Joshua

Specific Adaptations:

Curriculum & Time - No adaptations needed
Manipulatives -
   Tyler will use actual items (pencils, crayons, boxes) & a calculator
  Amy will use bingo chips to build arrays.
Amount -
   Tyler & Amy will write one problem
  Emily & Joshua will write more problems if time allows.

TIPS FROM TEACHERS

■ Encourage the use of regular classroom tools during assessment—rulers, blocks, calculators, and so on.

■ Give group tests regularly, so students will learn to discuss mathematics and to support one another.

■ Be alert to vision problems, hearing loss, muscular difficulties, or other physical problems.

■ Read to students who come from a culture with a strong oral tradition, or use a "multimedia" approach with them.

■ Preview assessments to familiarize students with the process.

■ Present questions or problems orally, in writing, and visually at the same time.

■ Brainstorm with other teachers or parents for alternative ways to express certain terms that may not translate well into another language.

■ Believe that all students can and should succeed. Let them know that they can.

Equity and Special Needs

READ ABOUT...

■ *Read about assessing students with special needs in "Assessing Mathematics Learning for Students with Learning Differences," by Lee Cross and Michael Hynes (1994).*

■ *Read about developing equitable assessment practices in "Assessment and Equity," by Terri Belcher, Grace Dávila Coates, José Franco, and Karen Mayfield-Ingram (1997), and in* Multicultural and Gender Equity in the Mathematics Classroom: The Gift of Diversity, *edited by Janet Trentacosta (1997).*

FIG. 3.16 (continued)

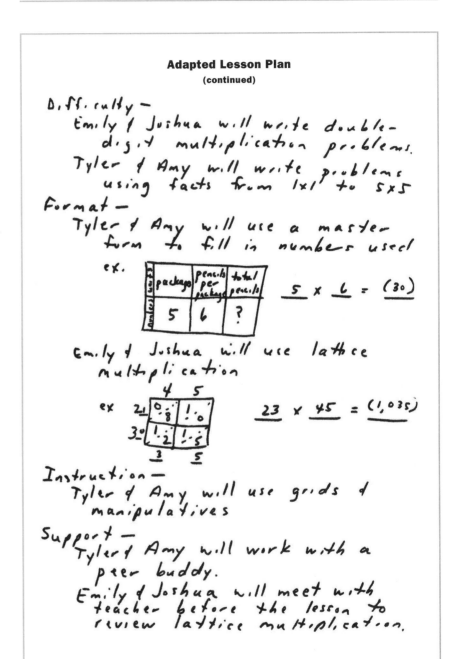

Adapted Lesson Plan
(continued)

Difficulty—
  Emily & Joshua will write double-digit multiplication problems.
  Tyler & Amy will write problems using facts from 1x1 to 5x5

Format—
  Tyler & Amy will use a master form to fill in numbers used
  ex.

packages	pencils per package	total pencils
5	6	?

  $\underline{5} \times \underline{6} = \underline{(30)}$

  Emily & Joshua will use lattice multiplication
  ex.

  $\underline{23} \times \underline{45} = \underline{(1,035)}$

Instruction—
  Tyler & Amy will use grids & manipulatives

Support—
  Tyler & Amy will work with a peer buddy.
  Emily & Joshua will meet with teacher before the lesson to review lattice multiplication.

Assessment beyond the Classroom

WHAT OTHER ASSESSMENT PROGRAMS HAVE AN EFFECT ON MY CLASSROOM ASSESSMENT?

Although this book is concerned with classroom assessment, it is important for professionals to be well-informed about other assessments. If possible, teachers should become involved in order to share their professional judgment.

National and International Assessments

In recent years several attempts have been made in the United States to promote a national assessment, or national tests. At this time, government-sponsored national assessments are not actively being developed, but they may become a concern in the future. The National Assessment of Educational Progress (NAEP), which conducts a periodic sampling from small groups of students of various ages across the country, issues occasional reports. This assessment uses performance tasks as well as typical test questions. Internationally, results from such efforts as the Third International Mathematics and Science Study (TIMSS) can help us know which areas were most difficult for our students.

Model Assessment Programs

Some states, provinces, and school districts have access to model assessment programs, such as that created by the New Standards program of the National Center on Education and the Economy (1997). This program suggests three components, all referenced to performance standards:

- On-demand tests, including basic-skills tests

- Samples of students' work with criteria, such as rubrics, for evaluating the work

- Ongoing assessment by teachers in the classroom, through observations, interviews, quizzes, and so forth

Materials provided by the New Standards program can be varied depending on local needs but may include multiple-choice questions, short tasks, longer tasks, and a portfolio program.

Another example of an assessment program is the Classroom Assessment Materials Project (CAMP), which is designed to be used by classroom teachers to assess students' achievement of the learning outcomes specified in the study program of the Province of Alberta, Canada. For each grade level, there is a teacher handbook with overview, scoring criteria, blackline masters for student tasks (multiple-choice and written-response questions, performance tasks, and number-facts tests), and examples of students' responses.

Assessment Beyond the Classroom

State and District Testing

READ ABOUT...

■ *Read about a teacher whose class-room assessment was affected by a state-mandated assessment in "Primary Portfolios" in* Mathematics Assessment: Cases and Discussion Questions for Grades K–5, *edited by William S. Bush (2001).*

■ *Read about opinions about state assessments in the May-June 1998 issue of* Mathematics Education Dialogues, *published by the National Council of Teachers of Mathematics.*

Many states, provinces, and school districts purchase standardized tests for the purpose of comparing classroom, school, district, and statewide results. Teachers' involvement in the selection of those tests can ensure the best match to local curricula and teaching methods.

WHAT ARE THE IMPLICATIONS FOR ME AND MY STUDENTS?

If their students will participate in tests from outside the school, teachers may want to make changes in some of their classroom processes. If, for example, the state chooses to use multiple-choice items for a general assessment, teachers ought to prepare students for this kind of testing, without making it the central focus of the year's instruction. Students should have occasional experience in taking multiple-choice tests, with class discussion about the right and wrong answers. A good preparation exercise is to have students write multiple-choice tests themselves and explain why they used all the answer choices.

CHAPTER 3

Managing Time and Logistics

HOW CAN I MANAGE IT ALL?

You have decided to take the plunge and change assessment—but are you going to be tied to your assessment system twenty-four hours a day? The question most asked by both first-year and veteran teachers is, How do we manage it all? Unfortunately, there is not a set of steps to follow because teachers all have their own ways of doing things. Here are some things that might help.

- *Set realistic goals.* Relax! Nothing happens overnight. You know how much time you have in a day, so start slowly. Pick one piece to implement at a time, and add to the system as you feel comfortable.

- *Find a buddy.* Having a compassionate peer to talk with about both successes and failures goes a long way. Time-saving ideas can be developed and shared together.

- *Look over the curriculum.* Implementing an assessment system shouldn't require double duty. Some parts of the curriculum may be compatible with your ideas, and some recent mathematics texts include ideas for performance assessment. With the growing trend toward curriculum integration, many ideas for assessing mathematics can also be found in language-arts manuals.

- *Involve your students.* Your students will understand better if they are part of the process. They can date and file papers, write reflections, and self-assess. Time well spent!

- *Experiment.* No one comes up with the perfect system the first time. Sometimes a checklist is better suited to a situation than a detailed narrative. Don't waste time doing too much.

- *Don't reinvent the wheel.* Much has been written about assessment over the years. Go to a professional library and see what is already available. Professional organizations can help. You can check for experts in the building and district. You can get on the Internet and see where it takes you.

- *Build an adult support system within the classroom.* Elementary school students are active learners; they won't wait very long. More adult help in the room can come from high school student volunteers, community volunteers, parents, or a student teacher. These adults can do assessments or can work with some students while we do assessment with others.

- *Ask for help.* Students are also seen by the principal, teachers of special subjects, lunch aides, and others. They might help, since mathematics concepts relate to many situations in school.

Managing Time and Logistics

TIPS FROM TEACHERS

■ *Introduce assessment techniques one at a time, so that you and the students won't feel overwhelmed.*

■ *Observe or think about only a few students a day.*

■ *Don't score every paper every time.*

■ *Gather a single student's paper from each group for grading after groups understand that all members have to be able to represent the group.*

■ *Take turns grading papers from one or two groups each day.*

■ *Have students preassess their papers before turning them in.*

■ *Use peer assessment and self-assessment. Ask students to check their own or each other's work.*

■ *Have students keep a log of work scheduled and work done.*

■ *Look at a single aspect of all papers for the day—for example, check for complete explanations on Monday and organizing information on Tuesday.*

■ *If using a rubric, use fewer levels—maybe two or three.*

■ *Save a day or two of class time for students to put together their portfolios, with checklists of required papers and student-prepared tables of contents.*

■ *Have students underline or highlight the parts of their work they especially want you to review.*

■ *Borrow from other teachers or books—problems, rubrics, manipulatives, or other ideas.*

■ *Postpone complicated techniques like portfolios until you are ready.*

■ *Accept the fact that there is never enough time. Set priorities and keep it simple.*

CHAPTER 3

Managing Time and Logistics

Figure 3.17 shows a checklist of logistics issues that will help with time management as well as with the effectiveness of assessment. A full-page copy of the checklist can be found in chapter 5 (p. 139).

FIG. 3.17

Logistics Issues

Reflect on the following questions and answer yes or no. If you think you should take action, complete the last column by planning how you will accomplish this task.

Question	Yes	No	How will I do it?
Do I need detailed notes for each observation?			
Do I plan for assessment observations each day?			
Do I encourage my students to reflect on their work?			
Do I involve my students in the documentation? Do I date every piece of documentation?			
Do my students date every place of work? Do I provide my students with work folders?			
Do I have a centralized place for portfolios?			
Do I leave detailed plans for substitutes to follow?			
Do I have "emergency plans" for substitutes who may feel more comfortable with "traditional" plans?			
Do I assess, document assessment, and file papers throughout the marking period?			

Chapter 4

Using the Results of Assessment: What Do I Do with the Evidence?

I collected tasks and information all summer, and now that school has started I've used some of what I have, and I have quite a bit of student work. But I need to ask a few more questions before I get much further, because already the papers and notes are stacking up.

What can I see when I look at student work? What's the difference between scoring and grading? How do I inform parents about how well their children are doing? What about public relations (the school board, for instance)? What about reliability and validity (I know they're going to ask!)? How do I evaluate the whole assessment program?

Looking at Students' Work

In this chapter we will consider various aspects of using the results of assessment. Any decision or action we take begins with looking at students' work or observing students at work.

WHAT SHOULD I LOOK FOR IN STUDENTS' WORK?

This chapter includes many examples of students' work, some of which are accompanied by the teacher's comments and questions. Teachers look to see what students know and how they can help students progress. In looking at the students' work and reading the teachers' comments, consider these questions:

- What questions shall I ask to stimulate students' thinking?

- How can I help students improve their communication in mathematics?

- Do the students understand the concepts?

- Can the students organize data and explain it?

- Do the students have a systematic approach to problems?

- What kind of mathematical thinking is reflected?

- What are the differences in the ways students present their results?

- Are the questions themselves good enough to elicit the information I need?

- How much revision should students do to make this work better?

RECTANGLES AND SQUARES

The class and I had been talking about multiplication and had found the "basic facts" using tiles. We had discovered that we could make rectangular shapes with the tiles for all the multiplication facts. We had a discussion about squares (2×2 and 3×3) and agreed that all squares are rectangles but not all rectangles are squares.

Today they had this problem:

> **Julie arranged 24 blocks into a rectangular shape. Describe the rectangle she made. Explain why you think what you wrote is true. Are any other answers possible? Explain.**

Almost all the students drew diagrams. It was clear that they needed to learn more about descriptions and reasoning, but that will come as we work on it. Here are a few examples, with some questions to ask. Posing the questions helps me look at the papers with new eyes to try to figure out what will add to their thinking.

*Dana's response below (**fig. 4.1**) tells me that if I want to find out about representations of multiplication, I have to ask the right questions!*

I'll just check her understanding with "What other multiplication problems might use twenty-four blocks?"

FIG. 4.1

Julie arranged 24 blocks into a rectangular shape.

Describe the rectangle she made.

Explain why you think what you wrote is true.

 8 × 3

—A rectangle has four sides
—All are parellell
—Sometimes two sides are longer than the two others
—It has four vertices

Are any other answers possible? Explain.

There are billions of other rectangles. Some have more than one story-(layer) some are flat or very long others are shorter. A square is also a rectangle

Looking at Students' Work

*Keri seems to get the idea of factors and area (see **fig. 4.2**), but I could ask her, "How could you show that as a multiplication sentence?" When they talk in groups, the 3×8 rectangle should be discovered. Those factors were the ones that fewest students came up with.*

FIG. 4.2

Julie arranged 24 blocks into a rectangular shape.

Describe the rectangle she made.

Explain why you think what you wrote is true.

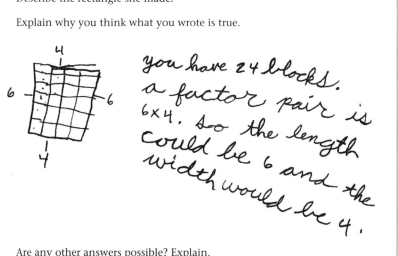

you have 24 blocks. a factor pair is 6×4. soo the length could be 6 and the width would be 4.

Are any other answers possible? Explain.

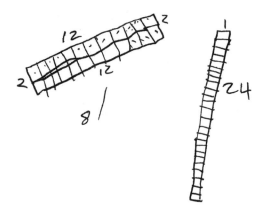

Looking at Students' Work

Chuck uses number sentences to connect the rectangles to multiplication (see fig. 4.3). I'd ask him, "How could you move these to put them in an order that shows a pattern?"

FIG. 4.3

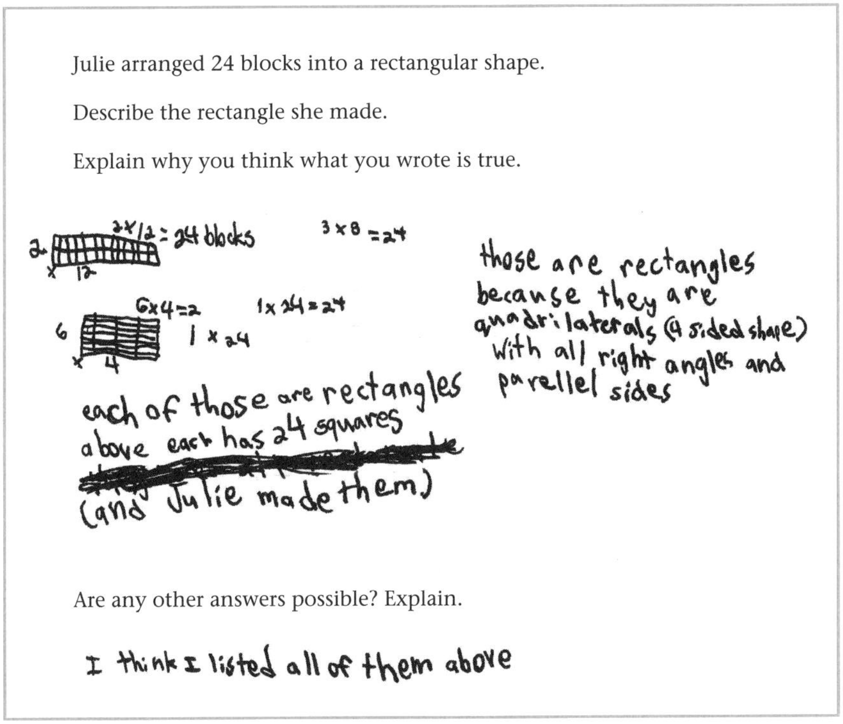

Julie arranged 24 blocks into a rectangular shape.

Describe the rectangle she made.

Explain why you think what you wrote is true.

2 [grid] $2 \times 12 = 24$ blocks $3 \times 8 = 24$
× 12

6 [grid] $6 \times 4 = 2$ $1 \times 24 = 24$
× 4 1×24

those are rectangles because they are quadrilaterals (4 sided shape) with all right angles and parellel sides

each of those are rectangles above each has 24 squares ~~and Julie made them.~~

Are any other answers possible? Explain.

I think I listed all of them above

Looking at Students' Work

*Lindsay's response (**fig. 4.4**) makes some good points. I'd ask her, "How can you be sure that you have all possible examples?"*

FIG. 4.4

Julie arranged 24 blocks into a rectangular shape.

Describe the rectangle she made.

Explain why you think what you wrote is true.

I think that a 4 by 6 would be best. It has 4 right (90° angles, parallel sides, and 2 pair of even sides that are different.

Are any other answers possible? Explain. *Yes!*

2 by 12 or 12 by 2
3 by 8 or 8 by 3
1 by 24 or 24 by 1

These are all factors of 24 & would ~~would~~ therefore make a rectangle because each factor pair have different numbers and would make different length sides.

Looking at Students' Work

INTUITIVE IDEAS OF ESTIMATING AND PREDICTING

I wanted to see what intuitive ideas my students had about using data to make predictions. I found the following task that seemed appropriate:

> **The class was looking at the number of raisins in little boxes of cereal. Here are the numbers the students found:**
>
> **15   13   19   14   15   15   22   16   14   18**
>
> **The teacher asked them to predict how many raisins would be in the next box opened. Explain how you would make a good prediction.**

The students' responses to this question revealed a wide range of logic. We have talked a little about this topic in class, but it appears that most students haven't had much experience. Let's look at some of the papers.

Duy's response (fig. 4.5) is very clear. I might ask to try to find another way of approaching the problem.

FIG. 4.5

The class was looking at the number of raisins in little boxes of cereal.

Here are the numbers the students found:

15   13   19   14   15   15   22   16   14   18

The teacher asked them to predict how many raisins would be in the next box opened.

Explain how you would make a good prediction.

To figure that out, I would add all the numbers that the class found raisins in little boxes of cereal, so I add 15 + 13 + 19 + 14 + 15 + 15 + 22 + 16 + 14 + 18 = 161 and divided by the number of how many numbers I add altogether, so I add 10 numbers, so now I divide 161 to 10 to find the average. 161 ÷ 10 = 16 R.1, so a good guess is 16.

Looking at Students' Work

*Jensen seems to be using the pattern of the last three numbers (see **fig. 4.6**). I'd ask, "What about all the other numbers? Do you need to include them?"*

FIG. 4.6

The class was looking at the number of raisins in little boxes of cereal.

Here are the numbers the students found:

    15   13   19   14   15   15   22   16   14   18

The teacher asked them to predict how many raisins would be in the next box opened. *20*

Explain how you would make a good prediction.

Because at the third end it is 16 and then 14 so it means that they add 2 and at the last one it is 18. and it means that they add 4 and cut my estimate 2 add 2 so if is 20.

---

*Devin seems to have used some of the ideas introduced when we worked on patterns (see **fig. 4.7**). How can I help students see the difference between one kind of question or problem and another? This is a lot like students' not knowing which operation to use in word problems. Context helps, but not always.*

FIG. 4.7

The class was looking at the number of raisins in little boxes of cereal.

Here are the numbers the students found:

15 ⟋2 13+6 19−5 14+1 15−0 15+7 22−6 16+2 14+4 18−3 15

The teacher asked them to predict how many raisins would be in the next box opened.

Explain how you would make a good prediction.

both sides might be the same so its probaly 15.

Looking at Students' Work

*Manuel used rounding (see **fig. 4.8**), but it's not clear that he understood the problem. I'd start out by reducing the problem to a simpler one. "If you had just three boxes and the first two contained fifteen raisins and thirteen raisins, what would you predict the third box would contain?"*

FIG. 4.8

The class was looking at the number of raisins in little boxes of cereal.

Here are the numbers the students found:

$$\frac{20}{15} \quad \frac{10}{13} \quad \frac{20}{19} \quad \frac{10}{14} \quad \frac{20}{15} \quad \frac{20}{15} \quad \frac{20}{22} \quad \frac{20}{16} \quad \frac{10}{14} \quad \frac{20}{18} \quad \frac{200}{160}$$

The teacher asked them to predict how many raisins would be in the next box opened. 200

Explain how you would make a good prediction.

I will round of each # to the nearest 10.

*Cyrill's strategy is similar to Devin's; however, he also looked for odd-even patterns (see **fig. 4.9**). He too needs to be encouraged to use a technique appropriate to the problem.*

FIG. 4.9

The class was looking at the number of raisins in little boxes of cereal.

Here are the numbers the students found:

15	13	19	14	15	15	22	16	14	18

The teacher asked them to predict how many raisins would be in the next box opened. 13

Explain how you would make a good prediction.

1st it 15 - 2 + 6 - 5 + 1 + 0 + 8 - 7 - 2 + 4 - 3

The variety of interpretations was fascinating. Our discussion will include some of the ideas the students had. We can talk about several ways of finding—for different purposes—answers to problems like this.

Looking at Students' Work

INVESTIGATIONS

We tried some beginning investigations today. I wanted to see what kinds of strategies the students used for estimating, as well as how well they organized and communicated, and how completely they could present their ideas. Here is the problem:

Estimate how many of one of these supplies we will use in our class this year. Choose one:

Pencils

Sheets of paper

Sheets of colored paper

Crayons

Describe what you were thinking and what you did to make your estimate.

Before they started, we talked about some facts they would need to know, such as that there are eighteen students in the class and thirty-six weeks in a school year. And then they jumped right in. I could see that they were trying very hard to put down as many ideas as they could. I wanted to be ready with some prompting or guiding questions.

*Rae's response about crayons (**fig. 4.10**) was simple and direct. Questions: Does each student have four packs, or is that for the whole class? What does the 6 × 4 mean?*

FIG. 4.10

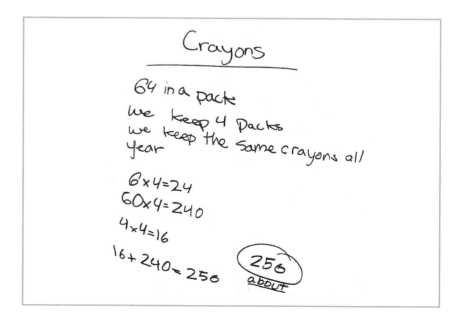

Crayons

64 in a pack
We keep 4 packs
we keep the same crayons all year

$6 \times 4 = 24$
$60 \times 4 = 240$
$4 \times 4 = 16$

$16 + 240 = 256$ 256 about

Looking at Students' Work

Eli chose pencils and went through what seemed like a sensible process (see **fig. 4.11**). Question: What if you get out forty pencils, or forty blocks, and see whether that looks like the number of pencils that you really use at school? (We need to do more work with using diagrams to help make more sense of the problem.)

FIG. 4.11

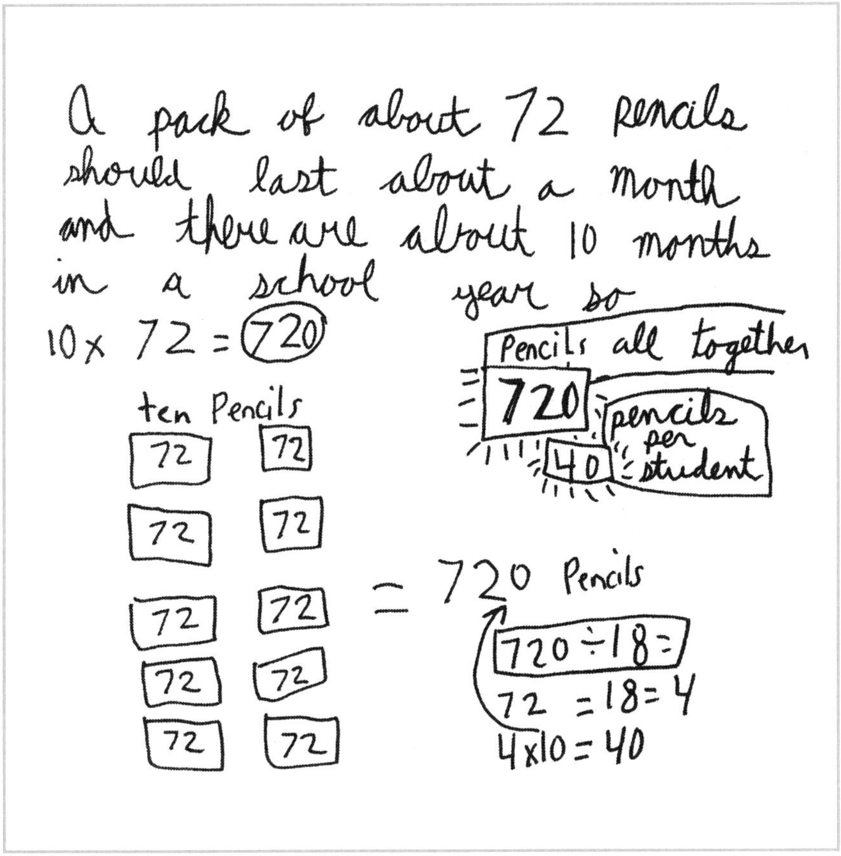

A pack of about 72 pencils should last about a month and there are about 10 months in a school year so

$10 \times 72 = \boxed{720}$

ten Pencils

| 72 | 72 |
| 72 | 72 |

| 72 | 72 | = 720 Pencils
| 72 | 72 |
| 72 | 72 |

Pencils all together

720 pencils per student

40

720 ÷ 18 =
72 = 18 = 4
4 × 10 = 40

Looking at Students' Work

Ariel started out well, but the calculations didn't seem to make sense (see fig. 4.12). Question: Use smaller numbers to make the problem simpler. How did you get your answer?

FIG. 4.12

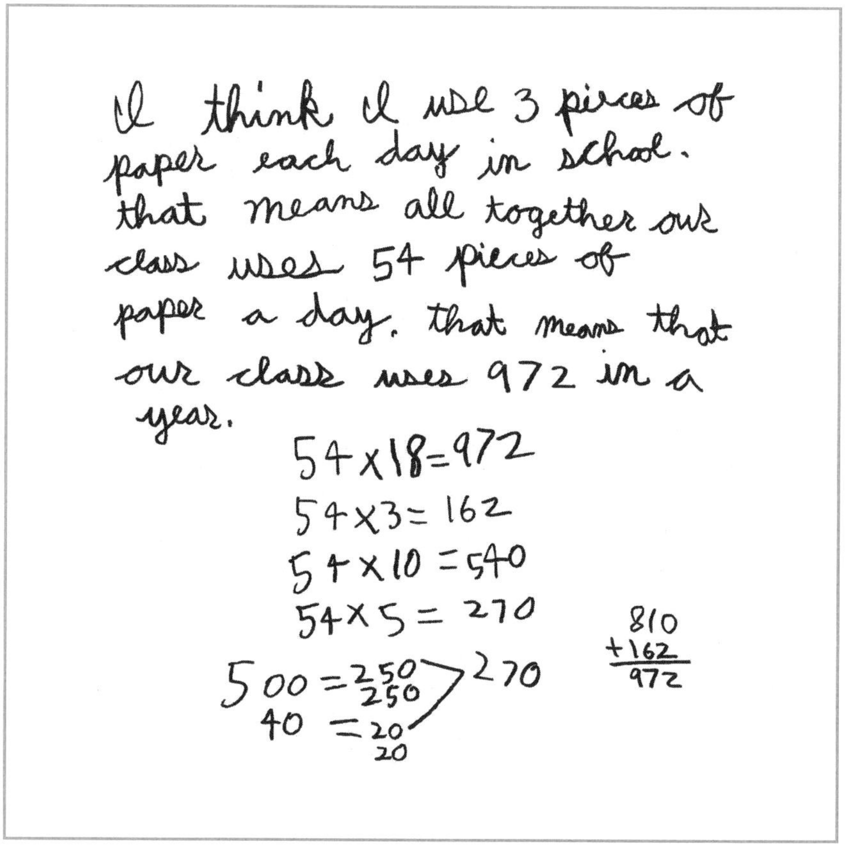

I think I use 3 pieces of paper each day in school. that means all together our class uses 54 pieces of paper a day. that means that our class uses 972 in a year.

$$54 \times 18 = 972$$
$$54 \times 3 = 162$$
$$54 \times 10 = 540$$
$$54 \times 5 = 270$$

$$500 = \begin{matrix} 250 \\ 250 \end{matrix} \Big\rangle 270$$
$$40 = \begin{matrix} 20 \\ 20 \end{matrix}$$

$$\begin{matrix} 810 \\ +162 \\ \hline 972 \end{matrix}$$

Looking at Students' Work

Alexis asked how many sheets of paper were in a package, and then she did her calculations (see **fig. 4.13**). I'm not sure of some of her logic. Questions: Why did you divide 36 by 2? What is the connection between the number of weeks and the number of students? How many sheets do you think each person uses in a month? A year?

FIG. 4.13

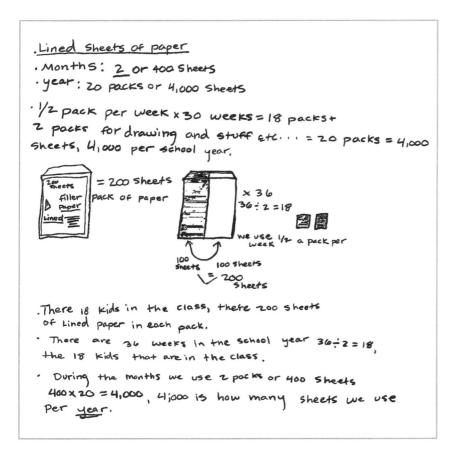

Tomorrow I'm going to ask the students who chose the same material to work in groups, talk together about their estimates, and then make oral presentations to the class. I'm hoping that the students will ask the questions that I would like to ask—and more of their own.

READ ABOUT...

■ *Read about* teachers confused by their students' work in "The New Student," "Melanie's Place-Value Understanding," and "When the Wrong Way Works" in Mathematics Assessment: Cases and Discussion Questions for Grades K–5, edited by William S. Bush (2001).

Looking at Students' Work

RACE TO THE FLAGPOLE

Sometimes I have to have students work on a question or problem before I can see the snags in it. Here is an example:

> **Three boys raced to the flagpole. The first one got there in 20 seconds. The second got there in half that time. The third got there in half of the second boy's time. What were their three times, and how did you figure them out?**

The results of four students' work are shown in **figures 4.14** *through* **4.17**.

FIG. 4.14

```
1  20
2  10
3   5

20 ÷ 2 = 10 ÷ 2 = 5
```

FIG. 4.15

The three times are twenty, ten, and five. I knew that because if you minus ten from twenty, it will still be ten so ten is half of twenty. Then you minus five from ten, it would still be five so that means five is half of ten.

Looking at Students' Work

FIG. 4.16

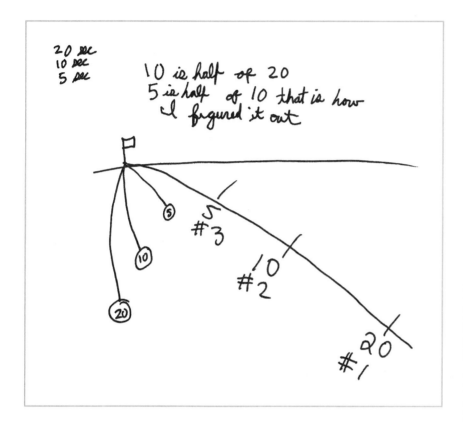

FIG. 4.17

I can see that both the students and I need to do more critical thinking about questions and their answers. In this case, when I came to the third student's diagram, I realized that the times had been listed in a backward fashion, so that "first" implied the winner even though that boy took longer to get there! How could I have missed the fact that in a race, the shortest time is the winner?

Of course, the students all dutifully worked out the arithmetic and didn't question the situation! It's a sloppy habit for them and for me. It's a good chance to talk about this, and I think I'll have them help me rewrite the problem so it makes sense. We can talk more about the meaning of "half" at the same time; a few of them seemed to have a little trouble with the second division.

Looking at Students' Work

MORE THAN ONE ANSWER

Before we tried this problem, we read a Curious George book, and I talked with the groups to be sure they all knew what bicycles and tricycles look like. Sometimes I forget that not all students have the same experiences.

> **Curious George collected bicycle and tricycle wheels. He had already found 6 wheels, and then he found 3 more. Draw a picture of how many bicycles and tricycles George could make. Explain why there might be more than one answer.**

The answers varied. Most of the students did find more than one answer. Some examples are shown in **figures 4.18** *through* **4.24.**

FIG. 4.18

He could make 2 tricycles and
1 bike and and
he could make three tricyeles.

FIG. 4.19

Georgp could make no bicks or
tricycles becaus he dos'in have
any spare parts.

Looking at Students' Work

FIG. 4.20

He could make 1 tricycle because
a tricycle has 3 weeles
He could make 3 bicycles
because a bicycles have 2 weeles
and it said George found 6 weeles so
if you cant by twos you would end
up with 3 bicycles.

bicycles   bicycles   bicycles   tricycle

Another way to solve it is this ↓

wheels bicycle   bicycle   tricle
6 wheel

FIG. 4.21

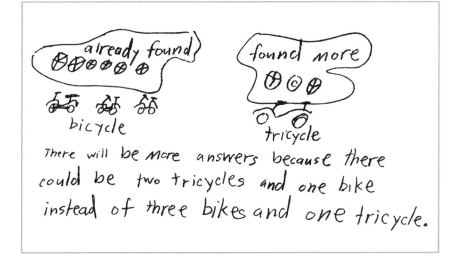

already found   found more

bicycle   tricycle

There will be more answers because there
could be two tricycles and one bike
instead of three bikes and one tricycle.

Looking at Students' Work

FIG. 4.22

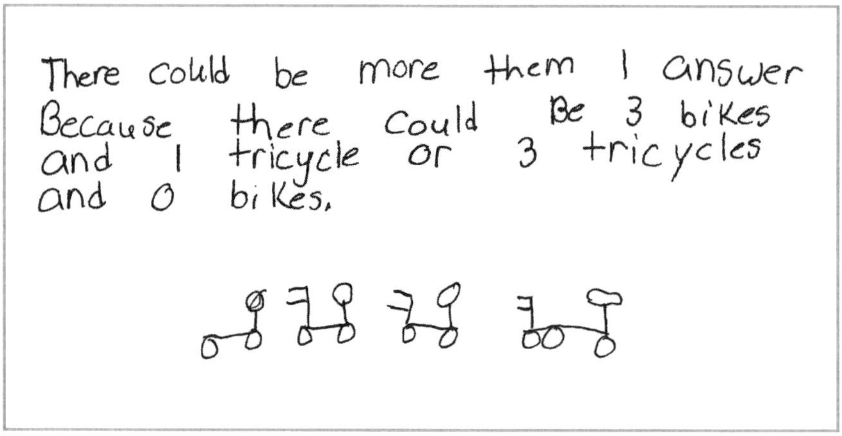

There could be more them 1 answer
Because there could Be 3 bikes
and 1 tricycle or 3 tricycles
and 0 bikes.

FIG. 4.23

There can be 1
Tricycle and 3 bicycles
because There Were 9
Wheels all together and
a tricycle has three
Wheels and a bicycle
has 2 Wheels

of tricycle | Number of Bicycles
3 Bicycles

Number
1 tricycle

Looking at Students' Work

FIG. 4.24

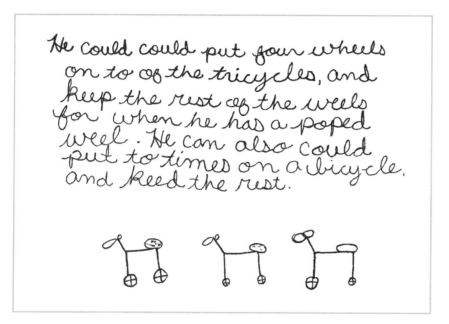

Some of the questions I plan to ask are these:

- *How could you be sure you had all the possible ways to make bicycles and tricycles? What kind of system would you use?*

- *What if you made all bicycles or all tricycles?*

- *What else would you really need to make bicycles or tricycles? (See the answer in **fig. 4.19**, which points out that he could make none because there were no other parts!)*

- *What if he had found ten wheels?*

- *Is there any number of wheels that could not all be used to make bicycles and tricycles? What if he had ninety-nine wheels?*

- *Does your diagram show all the wheels?*

- *Does this problem make sense to you? What do you know about bicycle and tricycle wheels that makes this problem silly?*

Looking at Students' Work

A PLANNING CHART

How Can I Organize What I See?

Collecting information about students is important; however, unless it is organized to uncover patterns of misconceptions and errors or to communicate to others, it may result in a lot of work for little gain. Some teachers have found that keeping individual folders on students, using daily or weekly checklists noting student performance or attitudes, or entering information about students into computer databases helps them organize the information.

I decided to find out how much my students knew about subtraction. I asked the students to describe how they would teach a little cousin to subtract two-digit numbers. They were asked to write out what they would say and give examples of problems. I wanted to find out—

■ *whether they described one strategy for numbers up to 10, and another strategy for numbers greater than 10;*

■ *whether they chose examples that required regrouping;*

■ *whether they gave more than one example;*

■ *whether they used both numbers and words;*

■ *whether they used diagrams or suggested using manipulatives;*

■ *whether the directions were clear enough to teach basic two-digit subtraction.*

Figures 4.25 *through* **4.33** *are responses from nine different students.*

FIG. 4.25

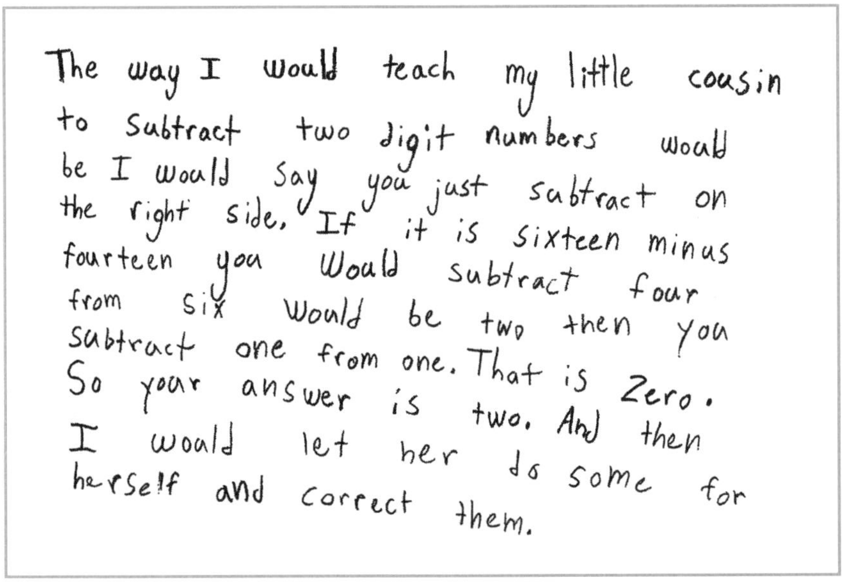

The way I would teach my little cousin to subtract two digit numbers would be I would say you just subtract on the right side. If it is sixteen minus fourteen you would subtract four from six would be two then you subtract one from one. That is Zero. So your answer is two. And then I would let her do some for herself and correct them.

CHAPTER *4*

Looking at Students' Work

FIG. 4.26

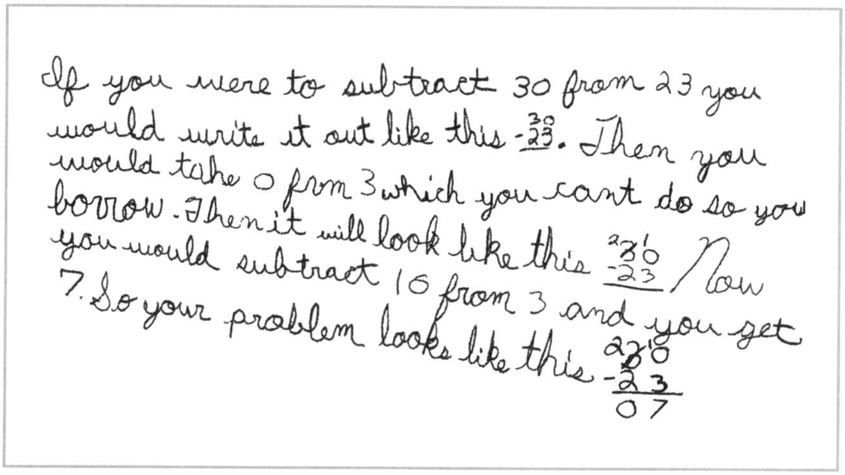

If you were to subtract 30 from 23 you
would write it out like this $\begin{array}{r}30\\-23\\\hline\end{array}$. Then you
would take 0 from 3 which you cant do so you
borrow. Then it will look like this $\begin{array}{r}{}^{2}\not{3}{}^{1}0\\-23\\\hline\end{array}$ Now
you would subtract 10 from 3 and you get
7. So your problem looks like this $\begin{array}{r}{}^{2}\not{3}{}^{1}0\\-23\\\hline 07\end{array}$

FIG. 4.27

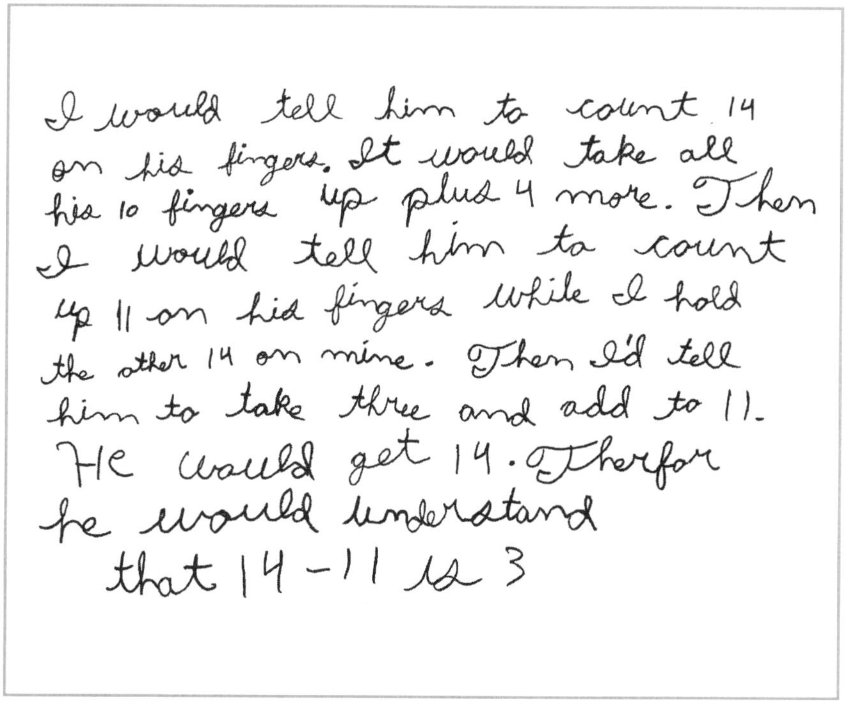

I would tell him to count 14
on his fingers. It would take all
his 10 fingers up plus 4 more. Then
I would tell him to count
up 11 on his fingers while I hold
the other 14 on mine. Then I'd tell
him to take three and add to 11.
He would get 14. Therfor
he would understand
that 14 − 11 is 3

Looking at Students' Work

FIG. 4.28

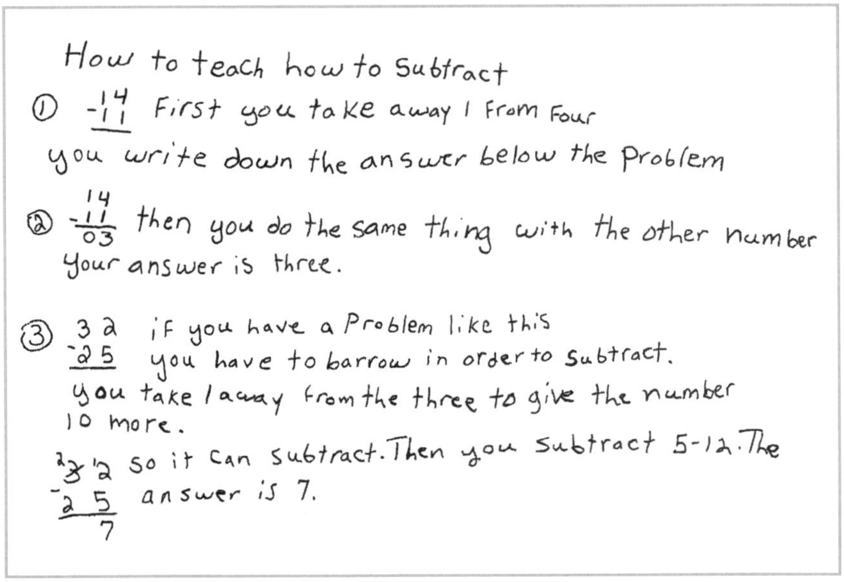

How to teach how to Subtract

① $-\frac{14}{11}$ First you take away 1 from Four

you write down the answer below the Problem

② $-\frac{14}{11}$ / 03 then you do the same thing with the other number

Your answer is three.

③ $\frac{3\,2}{-25}$ if you have a Problem like this
you have to barrow in order to subtract.
you take 1 away from the three to give the number
10 more.

$\frac{\overset{2}{\cancel{3}}\,^1 2}{-2\,5} / {7}$ So it can subtract. Then you subtract 5-12. The
answer is 7.

FIG. 4.29

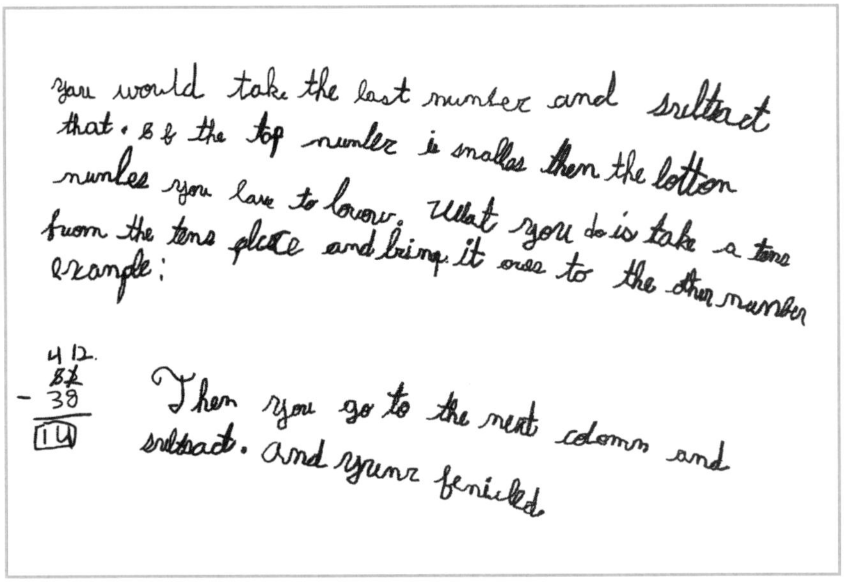

You would take the last number and sultract that. If the top number is smaller then the bottom number you have to borrow. What you do is take a tens from the tens place and bring it over to the other number example:

$\frac{\overset{4}{\cancel{5}}\,12}{-\;3\,8} / \boxed{14}$ Then you go to the next column and sultract. And your finished

FIG. 4.30

First I would show her a problem $\begin{array}{r}55\\-34\\\hline\end{array}$ then I would ask her what five take away four is. Then I would tell her to put the answer under the 4, $\begin{array}{r}55\\-34\\\hline 1\end{array}$ Then I would ask her what five take away three is, and her to put the answer under the 3, $\begin{array}{r}55\\-34\\\hline 21\end{array}$ and then go over the routine again with diffrent numbers. I would go over the routine many times until she under stood perfectly.

FIG. 4.31

First, take the number at the top on the right. If it is smaller then the the bottom right number then you must borrow. To borrow take ten away from the tens column. Add ten to the ones column. Now subtract the bottom right number from the top right number. Do the same with the tens column.

Looking at Students' Work

FIG. 4.32

First I'd get flash cards. Then I'd sit my
cousin down in a quiet place with no distractions
I'd also get a sheet of paper and a pencil
I'd go though the flashcards with him a
couple of times. Then if he didn't get it
I'd tell him to always start on the right
side. If the top number was smaller I'd
teach him how to borrow by taking one
away from the top left side and giving it
to the top right side. Then if he already
knew how to substract he could do the problem.
If he didn't get it I'd buy him a
calculator for his birthday.

FIG. 4.33

IF You havc 20 pieces of candy and you
eat 10 how many would you havc
Left? you can draw tnc pieces
of candy out or use yourn
fingers to explain to yourn
cousin 20 candies

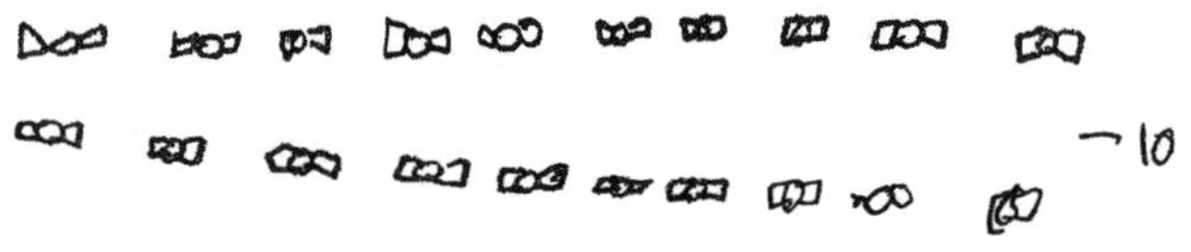

candies = 10
candies

Looking at Students' Work

When I went through the papers carefully, I had trouble seeing the whole picture, so I got out my class-list "blanks" (see the blackline master on p. 140) and made up a check sheet. **Figure 4.34** *shows some of my recordings. From the chart, I got a better idea of which concepts needed most time and work. I'll continue to use this information as we work through the topic.*

FIG. 4.34

PRE-ASSESSMENT – SUBTRACTION

On the following day, I started the students out in groups and asked them to explain their ideas to one another. I also asked them to discuss whether they thought everybody should do subtraction the same way or whether they should learn several ways to do it.

Homework that night was a page of subtraction problems. They were also asked to have their parents or other adults explain how they did subtraction when they were in school.

The next day we had a whole-class discussion about how they did the problems and what their groups had decided about using a single method or several. They agreed that they probably should know several ways to do subtraction, since all the ways they talked about had made sense. They did feel, though, that there was one "really right" way to do subtraction. We may talk about this again later in the year.

As I listened to what they said during the discussions, I took notes to be entered onto the chart. I think this will help me with a systematic plan.

READ ABOUT...

■ *Read about teachers looking at students' work in "A Room with More than One View," by Jean K. Stenmark, Pam Beck, and Harold Asturias (1994).*

Scoring and Grading

READ ABOUT...

■ *Read about scoring and grading in "Scores and Grades: What Are the Problems? What Are the Alternatives?" by Judith S. Zawojewski and Richard Lesh (1996).*

■ *Read about a middle school teacher's struggle with grading in "Does This Count for a Grade" in* Mathematics Assessment: Cases and Discussion Questions for Grades 6–12 *(Bush 2000).*

■ *For more tips about grading, read* Mathematics Assessment: Myths, Models, Good Questions, and practical Suggestions, *edited by Jean Stenmark (1991).*

WHAT IS THE DIFFERENCE BETWEEN SCORING AND GRADING?

Scoring is comparing students' work to criteria or rubrics that describe what we expect the work to be. *Grading* is the result of accumulating scores and other information about a student's work for the purpose of summarizing and communicating to others. In other words, students' work that is gathered through assessment can be scored, then the scores—along with other records—can help to determine grades.

Scoring in a more balanced assessment system has a more comprehensive meaning than the percent of correct responses on a test. When students write explanations of how they did a task or why they think their answer is appropriate, teachers must use different bases, such as rubrics, to evaluate the responses. Scores can be averaged just as we have done with percent scores, or weighted and then averaged if some tasks are considered more important than others. We can still indicate to students that, for example, 40 percent of their grade will come from daily work and papers turned in, 35 percent will come from assessment papers and tests, and 25 percent will come from class participation and oral reports. If we are using portfolios, part of the grade will come from the portfolios.

WHAT ARE CRITERIA AND RUBRICS?

Criteria describe more fully the intent of a standard. For example, a standard might say, "Students should understand computation and be able to add, subtract, multiply, and divide whole numbers accurately."

Examples of supporting criteria, or expectations, for division follow:

■ Students will accurately divide a three-digit number by a one-digit number and clearly explain the difference between problems that require regrouping and those that do not.

■ Students will show the relation between division problems and their multiplication counterparts.

■ Students will create reasonable word problems that use division.

Rubrics give still more detail, explaining the differences between different levels of success in completing a particular task. For example, consider this division problem:

> **Divide 129 by 7. Show all your work, and explain why your answer is correct. Use diagrams or drawings if possible. Then write a word problem that uses this division problem.**

CHAPTER *4*

Scoring and Grading

A rubric for this division task might look like this:

Level 3—Successful Response

- Arithmetic is complete and correct with work shown.

- Explanations are clear and show an understanding of the concept.

- Diagrams or drawings make sense in the context of the problem.

- Student-generated word problems are reasonable and can be solved using division.

Level 2—Partial Response

- Answers have minor computational errors that need to be corrected.

- Explanations, diagrams, or drawings are used but not clear.

- Word problems need additional information to be solved or do not use division.

Level 1—Needs Reteaching

- Answers have major computational mistakes or are incomplete. Work may not be shown.

- Explanations are missing or off target.

- Word problems are missing or not appropriate.

A rubric helps teachers analyze and score students' work by describing the levels of success. Usually at least three levels are described, sometimes more.

- Level 4—Above expectations, outstanding

- Level 3—Meets expectations, acceptable

- Level 2—Needs revision or more work

- Level 1—Shows need for reteaching

Rubrics may be very detailed like the previous one or they may be very simple and straightforward. Again, the main difference between criteria and rubrics is that rubrics describe levels of performance. Looking at the rubric, the teacher decides where a particular student's response fits. Often, some papers won't clearly fall into one category or another, but in a classroom the appropriate level can often be clarified by asking the student another question.

Scoring and Grading

READ ABOUT...

■ *Read about the concerns a group of teachers have with their students scoring work using a teacher-designed rubric in "A Difference of Opinion" in* Mathematics Assessment: Cases and Discussion Questions for Grades 6–12 *(Bush 2000).*

■ *Read about teachers' problems in agreeing on criteria for scoring student work in "Right or Wrong" in* Mathematics Assessment: Cases and Discussion Questions for Grades 6–12 *(Bush 2000).*

WHAT TYPES OF RUBRICS CAN BE USED?

A rubric may be *general* or *specific* and may also be *holistic* or *analytic*. General rubrics describe the qualities of successful work in terms applicable to any problem. Task-specific rubrics may reflect some elements of the general rubric but tend to focus on specific criteria for a given task. For example, for a task that relates percents to fractions, the general rubric might say, "Calculations are correct and appropriate," whereas a task-specific rubric could say, "Student recognizes and uses relations between percents and fractions (50% to 1/2 and 33$\frac{1}{3}$% to 1/3) in making calculations."

A teacher might use a general rubric to review a sample of papers for a task, then add details and develop a task-specific rubric to evaluate the entire set of responses. Specific rubrics can make assigning scores easier, faster, and more consistent. Sometimes a rubric will contain such information as a complete chart of all possible answers for the problem, a description of the mathematics involved, or a list of possible techniques students might use.

A holistic rubric describes the qualities of performance for each performance level. Students receive the single score for the level they have reached. Work is judged on its overall quality. An analytic rubric assigns scores to the components of the task. Those scores are then combined to make an overall score. **Figures 4.35** and **4.36** are examples of holistic and analytic rubrics.

FIG. 4.35

A Holistic Rubric

4 Fully accomplishes the purpose of the task.

Shows a good understanding and use of the main ideas of the problem.

Communicates thinking clearly, using writing, calculations, diagrams and charts, or other representations.

3 Substantially accomplishes the purpose of the task.

Shows a reasonable understanding and use of the main ideas of the problem.

Communicates thinking fairly well, but may use only one representation.

2 Partially accomplishes the purpose of the task.

Shows partial but limited grasp of the main mathematical ideas.

Recorded work may be incomplete, misdirected, or not clearly presented

1 Shows little or no progress in accomplishing the purpose of the task.

Shows little understanding of the main mathematical ideas.

Work is almost or completely impossible to decipher.

CHAPTER *4*

Scoring and Grading

FIG. 4.36

An Analytic Rubric, or Scoring Scale

Understanding the Problem	**0**	Complete misunderstanding of the problem
	1	Part of the problem misunderstood or misinterpreted
	2	Complete understanding of the problem
Planning a Solution	**0**	No attempt or totally inappropriate plan
	1	Partially correct plan based on part of the problem being interpreted correctly
	2	Plan could have led (or did lead) to a correct solution if implemented properly
Getting an Answer	**0**	No answer or wrong answer based on inappropriate plan
	1	Copying error; computational error; partial answer for a problem with multiple answers
	2	Correct answer and correct label for the answer

(From Charles, Lester, & O'Daffer (1987, p. 30)

Some experts have suggested weighting the relative values in the categories of analytic rubrics. For example, the three levels for "understanding the problem" and "planning a solution" might be worth 0, 3, and 6 points, so that those parts of the total score will affect the final score more than "getting an answer."

When an analytic rubric is used for formal assessment, such as that done by a state or province or a district, it is customary to give exactly the numbers of points shown in the rubric, with no partial values. This practice results in more consistent scoring. In a classroom, a teacher might modify this practice to allow for "in-between" papers or for special attributes of a student's work.

Scoring and Grading

KID-FRIENDLY RUBRIC

The Conejo Valley Unified School District in California developed a rubric for students to use. The full rubric is included in *Constructive Assessment in Mathematics: How to Get It Going in Your District*, from the California Mathematics Council (Anderson n.d.). **Figure 4.37** offers a shortened version of their rubric. Teachers should try to develop rubrics with their own students. See one teacher's story, later in this chapter, of developing standards that could become rubrics.

FIG. 4.37

LEVEL	6 Awesome, exceptional	4 Pretty good, gets the job done	2 Incomplete, confusing
UNDERSTANDING	■ Finds all important parts of problem ■ Fully understands math needed ■ Uses creative thinking	■ Finds most important parts of problem ■ Understands most of math needed	■ Little understanding of problem ■ Understands bits and parts of math needed
THINKING	■ Finds more than one way to solve problem ■ Uses diagrams, charts, graphs, etc. ■ Experiments and analyzes ■ Does more than the problem asks	■ uses only one way to solve problem ■ Some ways to show thinking may be missing ■ May experiment or analyze	■ Doesn't explain thinking ■ Uses ways to solve problem that don't fit the problem
COMMUNICATION	■ Writes a clear, convincing, thoughtful answer ■ Very clear diagrams	■ Addresses all parts of the problem ■ Writing may be unclear	■ Writes in a confusing way

From *Constructive Assessment in Mathematics: How to Get It Going in Your District* (Anderson n.d.)

Scoring and Grading

There are many other forms of rubric, or description of criteria. One example is found in Christina Myren's (1995) *Posing Open-Ended Questions in the Primary Classroom*. The levels, instead of representing scores, indicate "levels of understanding" and may be different for each lesson. For example, here is one of the problems.

> **5 children went home in cars. 2 children rode home on bikes. 2 children walked. How many wheels took the children home? Draw or write to explain your answer.**

Figure 4.38 illustrates the levels of understanding for this problem. Other categories could be added, such as these:

- The child shows more than one possible solution. (There could have been 5, 4, 3, or 2 cars—or 1 car if all rode in one car, so answers could range from 8 wheels to 24 wheels.).

- The child uses numbers or equations as well as pictures.

FIG. 4.38

The child depicts some wheels and children, but either does not address the mathematics or does not solve any part of the problem correctly.	The child depicts the correct number of children, but not a correct number of wheels; or the child depicts a correct number of wheels, but not the correct number of children.	The child depicts a correct number of both wheels and children to arrive at one possible solution to the problem.

From *Posing Open-Ended Questions in the Primary Classroom* (Myren 1995, pp. 24–25)

Scoring and Grading

For a problem that requires organizing information, the levels might be as in **figure 4.39**.

FIG. 4.39

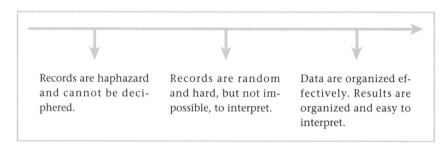

| Records are haphazard and cannot be deciphered. | Records are random and hard, but not impossible, to interpret. | Data are organized effectively. Results are organized and easy to interpret. |

From *Posing Open-Ended Questioins in the Primary Classroom* (Myren 1995, pp. 24–25).

Figures 4.40 and **4.41** offer other examples of a scoring profile and a rubric.

FIG. 4.40

SCORING CRITERIA FOR PERFORMANCE ASSESSMENT TASKS
Generalized Mathematics Holistic Scoring Criteria

	PROBLEM SOLVING	COMMUNICATION
3	■ Analyzes and readily understands the task. ■ Develops an efficient and workable strategy. ■ Shows explicit evidence of carrying out the strategy. ■ Synthesizes and generalizes the conclusion.	■ Rich, precise, and clear all the time (mathematically correct, correct symbolism). ■ Representation is very perceptive (chart, diagram, graph). ■ Explanations are logical and appropriate.
2	■ Understands the task. ■ Develops a workable strategy. ■ Infers (some evidence of a plan) but it is not always clear. ■ Connects and applies the answer.	■ Appropriate most of the time, accurate, mostly clear. ■ Representation is accurate and quite appropriate. ■ Explanations are mostly clear and logical.
1	■ Partially understands the task. ■ Uses appropriate strategy some of the time. ■ Possible evidence of a plan—not clear. ■ Partial connection of an answer.	■ Appropriate some of the time, but may not be clear. ■ Uses representation but not too precisely. ■ Explanations have some clear parts.
0	■ Totally misunderstands. ■ Inappropriate, unworkable strategy. ■ No evidence of carrying out a plan. ■ No connections to answer. ■ Blank.	■ Unclear or inappropriate use of symbolism. ■ Incorrect use of representation. ■ Explanation is not clear. ■ Blank.

These *Scoring Criteria* are *holistic*. For *Problem Solving* and for *Communication*, choose the score with descriptors that most closely exemplify a student's overall performance.

CHAPTER *4*

Scoring and Grading

FIG. 4.41

NEW STANDARDS™ Portfolio Scoring Profile ■ Mathematics ■ Elementary School

Student Code: _____	Date: _____	Reader Name: _____	Reader: One Two Three
			❏ ❏ ❏

Each step is a prerequisite for those that follow.

Step 1 Submitted: Has work been submitted for this entry?

Step 2 Readable: Can you read the student work and make sense of it?

Step 3 Fits the Definition: Is this the right kind of evidence for this entry/exhibit?

Step 4 Quality Judgment: Does it meet the criteria for the exhibit and entry instructions?

Mathematical Concepts Exhibit

One entry for each of the following:

	Step 1	Step 2	Step 3	Step 4	Mathematical Concepts Exhibit Criteria	Comments
Arithmetic and Number	❏	❏	❏	❏	❏ Important concept ❏ Used accurately ❏ Represented in multiple ways ❏ Explained the concept	
Geometry and Measurement	❏	❏	❏	❏	❏ Important concept ❏ Used accurately ❏ Represented in multiple ways ❏ Explained the concept	
Function and Algebra	❏	❏	❏	❏	❏ Important concept ❏ Used accurately ❏ Represented in multiple ways ❏ Explained the concept	
Statistics and Probability	❏	❏	❏	❏	❏ Important concept ❏ Used accurately ❏ Represented in multiple ways ❏ Explained the concept	

Scoring and Grading

HOW DO I USE RUBRICS TO SCORE STUDENTS' WORK?

In **figures 4.42–4.45** are four student papers produced in response to the following problem:

> **Molly needs some green paper for her art project. She can get 2 sheets for 4¢ at one store or 4 sheets for 6¢ at another store. Which is a better price? Explain your thinking at each step.**

FIG. 4.42

Name _____ *Jeanette* _____ Grade ___ 4th

Molly needs some green paper for her art project.

She can get 2 sheets for 4¢ at one store or 4 sheets for 6¢ at another store.

Which is a better price?

Explain your thinking at each step.

I think four sheets for 6¢ is better because if you run out of paper you still have some there to use

Scoring and Grading

FIG. 4.43

Name _Martha_   Grade _4_

Molly needs some green paper for her art project.

She can get 2 sheets for 4¢ at one store or 4 sheets for 6¢ at another store.

Which is a better price? _4 sheets for 6¢_

Explain your thinking at each step.

but 4 sheets be 6¢ If 2 sheets would be 4¢ I think she should go to the store that has 4 sheets for 6¢. because at the first store 2 sheets would be 4¢. that would mean 4 sheets would be 8¢.

FIG. 4.44

Name _Michael_   Grade _4_

Molly needs some green paper for her art project.

She can get 2 sheets for 4¢ at one store or 4 sheets for 6¢ at another store.

Which is a better price? _4 sheets for 6¢_

Explain your thinking at each step.

4 sheets is more than 2 plus it only cost 6¢

Scoring and Grading

FIG. 4.45

Name _Mashonna_   Grade _4_

Molly needs some green paper for her art project.

She can get 2 sheets for 4¢ at one store or 4 sheets for 6¢ at another store.

Which is a better price?   6¢

Explain your thinking at each step.

> First I tot a lot long and said the both are bad prices but then I said I don't know how many papers she need so I picked 6¢.

Try using the holistic rubric on page 120, the analytic rubric on page 121, and perhaps the kid-friendly rubric on page 122 to see what scores you award to the four papers. Before you begin to score, look at the problem to identify—

- the essential mathematics;

- the possible correct answers;

- the practical implications of the problem (for example, in this problem the number of pieces of paper needed is not known—students may or may not take this into account);

- what specifics, if any, you would add to the rubrics.

Then score the papers. Compare your scores with other teachers' and discuss the differences, both between your scores and theirs and between the results of holistic and analytic scoring. What do you think are the strengths and weaknesses of each rubric? How could you use the results?

Scoring and Grading

In **figure** 4.46 are some holistic and analytic scores that were given by others, for comparison. How do they compare with yours?

FIG. 4.46

Student	Holistic Score and Comments	Analytic Score and Comments (weighted score of 0, 3, or 6 for understanding and planning, and 0, 1, or 3 for correct answer)
Jeanette	**2**—Substantially accomplishes the task, recognizes getting more for amount of money, communication missing	Understanding—**3** (no price comparing) Planning—**0** (reasoning missing) Answer—**3**
Martha	**4**—Fully accomplishes the task shows a grasp of the concept, communication clear	Understanding—**6** Planning, interpretation—**6** Correct answer—**3**
Michael	**3**—Partial understanding of purpose of task, understood central idea. (Michael includes extra info that 4 is more than 2, does not explain.)	Understanding—**3** Planning—**3** Answer—**3**
Mashonna	**1**—Shows little or no progress, doesn't seem to be getting it. Needs reteaching.	Understanding—**0** Planning—**0** Answer—**3** (No reasoning given)

Note: Some people might want to rewrite this problem to remove the ambiguity about the number of sheets Molly needs, but possibly it shows more about the children's thinking this way. We want to look for more problems that will get at the practical point of view and that will lead children to point out that more information is needed. Such problems build their ability to recognize and define the assumptions that have to be made to solve some problems.

Scoring and Grading

A STORY OF STUDENTS AND CRITERIA

I wanted to start teaching my class about criteria so they would know a little more about how to evaluate their own work. But first I thought I'd find out what they thought good work looked like. **Figure 4.47** *shows what they came up with. From their description, we made a poster to put up on the wall. I almost asked them whether the ideas were in order, with the most important at the top, but I wanted them to feel ownership, so we left it the way they wrote it. We used these criteria every day for a month or so. Of course, these criteria had always been part of what the kids knew was expected, but somehow it helped to have them formalized and made visible. The students did start paying more attention to what they were doing. We even sent the list home in a letter to parents.*

FIG. 4.47

Good Work

The answer is right.

The paper is neat, with your name and the date.

All the words are spelled right.

All parts of the problem are done; nothing is left out.

The math has all been done.

All the work is shown.

One day, a group felt that they had some papers that were so good they should get extra credit, so they came up with the idea of making a poster for "super work." **Figure 4.48** *shows what they added. This time I couldn't resist intervening, so I asked them to add, "The person used a system and organized the work well." They said OK, but I'm not sure they all knew what they were agreeing to! Somebody suggested that we should make the posters into a checklist that they could keep in their desk or take home, so we did that. At that time I asked them to consider which things were most important, so they changed the order a little, but not much. Having the answer right was still number 1.*

CHAPTER *4*

Scoring and Grading

FIG. 4.48

Super Work

The paper uses diagrams, numbers, and words to explain the answer.

The person has made the paper interesting, with colored pens and pencils or decorations.

There are very logical explanations.

The person has done more than the problem needed. They might have used bigger numbers or said, "If I changed this number here, then this would happen to the other numbers," or something.

The person told how the work was checked.

The person made an oral report that was very clear.

About halfway through the year, when parent conferences were coming up, I asked the students what we could do for new people who didn't know about our lists. I explained that their plan would also be a big help in talking to parents, who want specific suggestions about how they can help. They talked it over in student groups and came up with the idea of making a list of helpful suggestions for doing good work. The results are shown in **figure 4.49.**

FIG. 4.49

Helpful Suggestions

____Check your arithmetic.

____Be neater—use lined paper.

____Be sure you show all your work.

____Explain how you got your answer.

____Try to find another answer. There might be more than one.

____Look on the list of strategies to see if one world work.

____Get out your math book and study these pages: _____.

____Ask your group to help you say what you mean.

____Have your partner or your group help you organize.

____Look at some other good work to see what is different from yours.

____Ask the teacher to explain the ideas again.

READ ABOUT...

■ *Read about teachers scoring students' work in "A Team Approach" and "Scoring Student Work with Colleagues" in* Mathematics Assessment: Cases and Discussion Questions for Grades K–5, *edited by William S. Bush, (2001), and in "Right or Wrong" in* Mathematics Assessment: Cases and Discussion Questions for Grades 6–12, *edited by William S. Bush (2000).*

■ *Read about a teacher who uses a rubric to explain students' progress to parents in "A Rubric Solves My Problem" in* Mathematics Assessment: Cases and Discussion Questions for Grades K–5, *edited by William S. Bush (2001).*

■ *Read about developing and using rubrics in "Assessing Mathematical Processes: The English Experience," by Malcolm Swan (1996), and in "Assessing Problem-Solving Thought Processes," by Annette Ricks Leitze and Sue Tinsley Mau (1999).*

■ *Read about refining rubrics in "So Math Isn't Just Answers," by Kari Brown-Herbst (1999).*

■ *Read about scoring students' work in "Cooperative Problem Solving: But What about Grading?" by Diana L. Kroll, Joanne Masingila, and Sue Tinsley Mau (1992).*

Scoring and Grading

READ ABOUT...

■ *Read about teachers who involve students in developing rubrics in "Show and Tell," "Primary Portfolios," and "Students as Assessor" in* Mathematics Assessment: Cases and Discussion Questions for Grades K–5, *edited by William S. Bush (2001).*

Next, I brought in some rubrics and criteria from other places. When the students looked at those, they said they thought ours were better, and I agreed, so we used our own for the rest of the year. They really used the lists to assess their papers. They would trade papers with another group and judge one another's work. They took it very seriously, especially the notion of being helpful instead of critical. There was a definite improvement in the quality of their work and in the quality of their interactions.

Of course, I still had the responsibility for grades. The good thing about that, though, was that I could use these same criteria for grading. I did use some quiz and test grades that had regular old-fashioned percent scores, but most of each report-card grade came from what students themselves had said work should be like. It really was a help with parent conferences, since we were all "on the same page." I'll surely do this again next year.

WHAT ARE RELIABILITY AND VALIDITY IN SCORING?

Important to everyone with an interest in any assessment system are its reliability and validity. *Reliability* refers to the ability of an assessment to give consistent results. *Validity* refers to the extent to which an assessment measures what it was designed to measure. In a classroom, validity might also be interpreted to mean the extent to which an assessment measures what we are teaching or what the students are learning—or perhaps what we *ought* to be teaching.

Portfolios and performance assessments are still being developed as means to assess and report progress to supplement or replace letter grades and standardized tests. We may not have proved to the satisfaction of all that these assessments improve learning or are a better choice than standardized tests. But their use is on the rise. Why? Because portfolios and performance assessment are closer to real-life situations. They reflect both the process and the product. Teachers can find out how students approach and carry out tasks, not just how many answers they get correct. These assessments actively involve students and should have a positive impact on classroom teaching. Instead of "teaching to the test," we can engage our students in meaningful experiences that go beyond memorizing facts and algorithms.

More research is needed to evaluate the effectiveness of new forms of classroom assessments. When students' work is assessed outside the classroom, as in statewide or districtwide tests, teachers can get experience in calibrating their judgments. Further research should also assure teachers that when they use clear criteria, performance assessment can be reliable.

HOW CAN I IMPROVE VALIDITY AND RELIABILITY IN SCORING STUDENTS' WORK?

It is important to score students' work as validly and reliably as possible. Some teachers have improved their scoring by considering the ideas in "Tips from Teachers" on this page.

CHAPTER *4*

Communicating with Parents

HOW CAN I COMMUNICATE MY ASSESSMENT RESULTS AND PRACTICES TO PARENTS?

We can involve parents in our early efforts to make changes in assessment by asking them what and how they would like their children to learn: What is important to this community? We might want to send them some examples of assessment ideas we are considering so they will know what's coming.

Parents can also be invited to participate in some assessments. For example, we might meet with a group of parents to explain to them how they can do an observation at home or in class with the help of a checklist of things to look for. Or parents can do an activity with the class while the teacher is observing students.

For end-of-unit presentations by groups of students, a panel of students and parents or other adults can serve as an evaluating board. They might want to meet ahead of time to decide on criteria or to agree on how the results will be used. This kind of activity gives prominence to what students do.

Other ways of informing parents might include the following:

■ Send home letters that explain goals or periodic newsletters with information about the classroom and samples of students' work.

■ Give them suggestions for how to help students be ready for assessments.

■ Suggest assessment questions parents can use with their children, such as "What strategies did you use?" or "What was the mathematics in this problem?" or "Please tell me about the problem in your own words."

■ Ask parents to help score students' papers using rubrics.

■ Give parents examples of multiple-choice, true-or-false, open-ended, and other kinds of questions on the same topic, so they can see the differences.

■ Have students present their portfolios to their parents, either at home or with the teacher present for questions and comments, perhaps during parent-teacher conferences.

Parents are accustomed to seeing traditional assessments used in the classroom. They will need to know why and how a change will benefit their children. Once they see the benefits, they could become the greatest advocates for the changes. Educators should keep the discussion with parents open, especially during an implementation year.

Communicating with Parents

READ ABOUT...

■ *Read about communicating with parents in* Getting Your Math Message Out to Parents, *by Nancy Litton (1998) and in "Parents, Portfolios, and Personal Mathematics," by Jacque Ensign (1998).*

■ *Read about an elementary school teacher whose students help her find a way to communicate what they know to their parents in "Show and Tell" in* Mathematics Assessment: Cases and Discussion Questions for Grades K–5, *edited by William S. Bush (2001).*

■ *Read about an elementary school teacher who has her students share their assessment results with their parents in "Student-Led Conferences" in* Mathematics Assessment: Cases and Discussion Questions for Grades K–5, *edited by William S. Bush (2001).*

Figure 4.50 illustrates a letter to parents explaining some transitions that a teacher is making in her assessment practices. Note how the teacher is preparing parents for these substantial changes.

FIG. 4.50

Dear Parents or Guardians,

Here is a copy of the results of the recent standardized test that your student took. Please review it, and if you have any questions, call me or the school office.

The form shows a "percentile" ranking. Percentile does not mean the percent correct. Rather, it represents a ranking on a scale of 1 through 99. If, for example, a child is in the 40th percentile, it does not mean he or she got 40% correct; it means that out of every 100 children who take the test, about 40 (or 40% of the children) will score lower and about 60 will score higher. Again, if you have any questions, please call.

Not all of a child's understanding can be reflected in test scores, so I am also sending a sample packet, or portfolio, of your child's work. Also enclosed is a copy of the general criteria we use for assessing the work in the portfolio. Next year we plan to make the portfolio program more formal.

Please ask your child to explain to you what the portfolio of work is and how it was put together. The children should be able to explain what each problem or question asks, how they worked to solve it, what the answers mean, and how their work was evaluated.

I find that when I say something about the positive aspects of work, it can be more motivating than "red ink," or pointing out mistakes, so you might consider looking first for positive comments you can make.

Ask your student to tell you what he or she needs to work on next or what he or she wants to improve. Doing so allows your student to take responsibility for the work. I have been encouraging students to revise most classwork to stress that doing their best work is important.

I look forward to seeing you again at the open house next month.

Sincerely,

Your child's teacher

CHAPTER *4*

Public Relations

HOW DO I PRESENT MY ASSESSMENT CHANGES TO THE SCHOOL COMMUNITY?

Before telling others about the changes that will happen, you should have the details straight so that you can present your information clearly, then listen and respond to the views of others. You can explain that you are interested in understanding more about students' learning with different kinds of assessment.

To present changes to administrators, you might meet with the principal first, and be prepared to answer the question, "Why is this better than what you do now?" You then might arrange for follow-up discussions about how the changes are going, what assistance the principal can provide, and when the principal can observe the benefits discussed. You can plan, for instance, to invite the principal to hear students make a group report and participate as other students ask questions about the group's work. You can ask the principal to come to a session with other teachers when you score students' papers and talk about what you are seeing and how students learn.

To present changes to other teachers, talk with them before you make the changes and give them examples of the kinds of problems and ways of assessing that you are talking about. Continue through the year to keep them informed of both your successes and your failures. You can invite them to review students' work, to come to scoring sessions, to hear classroom presentations, or to observe. Sharing among teachers about assessment can be a valuable in-service session.

To present changes to the community at large, you can offer to have your students make a presentation to the school board. Give each board member a checklist of ideas to watch for. You can have students write letters to the newspaper telling about what they are learning or invite newspapers to send a reporter to the school when you are finishing major projects that will be evaluated according to your new standards. You can send community members copies of the criteria students are using to judge their own work.

As it is with standards, criteria, rubrics, and assessment and with students' work itself, openness and involvement are the best policies.

Program Evaluation

Periodically, or at the end of a semester or year, take stock of what you are doing. Looking back to the planning described in chapter 3, ask yourself the following questions. For each, give specific examples, as if you were putting together an assessment portfolio for yourself.

- What was it I set out to do?
  - Have I done that?
  - Is that still what I want to do?
- What is the effect on the students?
  - Have the students become better problem solvers?
  - Has the quality of the students' responses improved?
  - Are more students receiving higher scores than at the beginning of the year?
  - Have the students' attitudes toward mathematics changed?
  - Have students become better at taking responsibility and assessing their own progress?
  - Do the students understand the importance of assessment?
- What am I learning?
  - Am I looking at the important parts of mathematics?
  - Have I learned helpful information about how the students learn?
  - Am I better able to look at the full range of students' ability levels?
  - Am I seeing things about the students that I didn't see before?
  - Have I created, clarified, and revised standards and criteria for good work?

CHAPTER *4*

Program Evaluation

- How has the implementation gone?
    - What assessment methods have I tried?
    - What others do I have specific plans for?
    - Are my questions and problems appropriate, challenging, and open for all students to respond to?
    - Have I arranged time and space to work on assessment?
    - Do the teachers think assessment is working well, or is it an added burden?
    - Do I have all the materials I need?
- Public relations
    - Have I convinced other staff members to reconsider their assessment practices?
    - Have I communicated well with parents?
    - Do the school and community support new assessments?
- Plans
    - What shall I focus on next?

It would be a good idea to look at only a few of these questions at a time. It may be discouraging to expect to have accomplished all the goals implied in these questions in a short time. You could start with a brainstorming session, asking "What have been the biggest benefits?" and "What has been most difficult?" Then look at a few practices, see what you want to continue as it is and what might need to be changed, and take action to bolster your efforts.

Adapted Lesson Plan

Objective:

Instructional Plan:

Assessment Plan:

Name(s) of student(s) needing lesson adaptations:

Specific Adaptations:

Logistics Issues

Logistics Issues

Reflect on the following questions and answer yes or no. If you think you should take action, complete the last column by planning how you will accomplish this task.

Question	Yes	No	How will I do it?
Do I need detailed notes for each observation?			
Do I plan for assessment observations each day?			
Do I encourage my students to reflect on their work?			
Do I involve my students in the documentation? Do I date every piece of documentation?			
Do my students date every place of work? Do I provide my students with work folders?			
Do I have a centralized place for portfolios?			
Do I leave detailed plans for substitutes to follow?			
Do I have "emergency plans" for substitutes who may feel more comfortable with "traditional" plans?			
Do I assess, document assessment, and file papers throughout the marking period?			

Class List

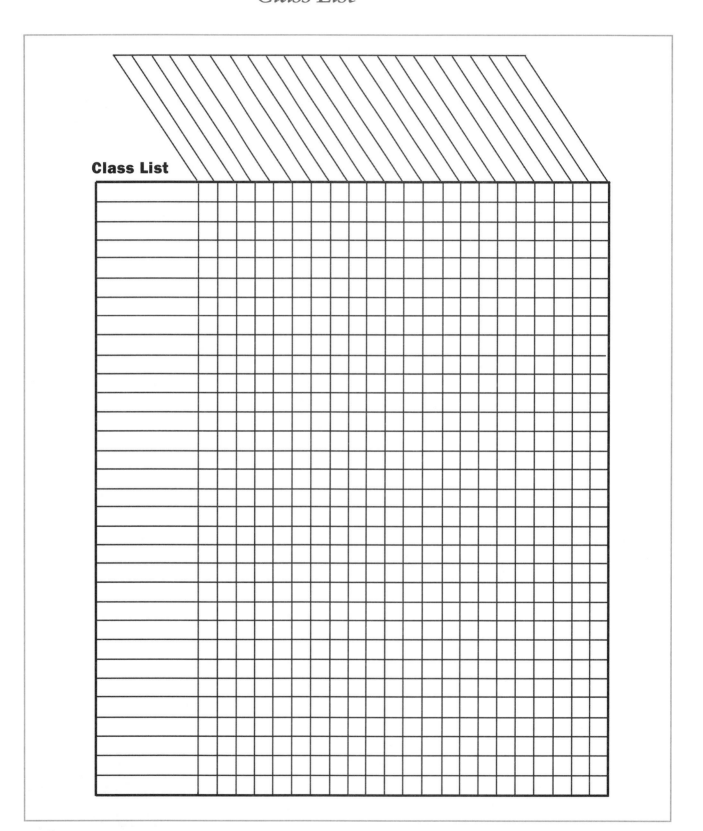

Class List

Magic Squares

Albrecht Dürer (1471–1528) was a famous German artist. He lived during the Renaissance and was one of the first to use the geometry of perspective in his work. His etching titled *Melancolia* contains the 4 × 4 magic square exactly as shown here. Notice how cleverly he incorporated the date 1514.

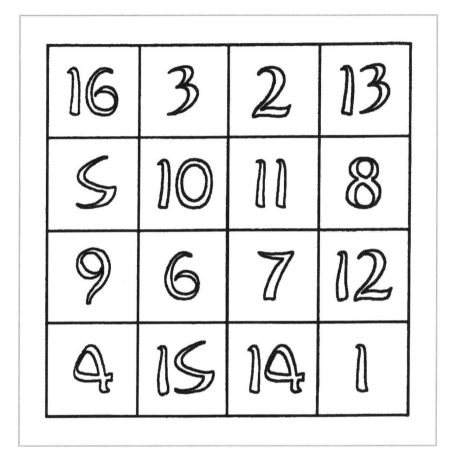

The numbers in every row, column, and diagonal of a magic square have the same magic sum.

1. What is the magic sum for this magic square?

2. How many rows, columns, and diagonals can you find with this magic sum?

3. Find five 2 × 2 squares in the magic square with four numbers that have the same sum as the magic sum.

4. Now try to find four numbers, each from a different row and column, that also have the same sum as the magic sum. There are two solutions besides the two diagonals.

From Maletsky (1985, p. 1)

New Students

Davis School is growing.

Two years ago there were 900 students.

Last year there were 10% more than two years ago.

This year there are 10% more than last year.

How many students does Davis school have this year?

Show all your work.

Black and Green

You have 12 blocks. There are 3 times as many black blocks as green blocks. Draw the 12 blocks, and mark B on the black ones and G on the green ones.

What fraction of the blocks are green?

What fraction are black?

Telephone Directions

Imagine that you are on the telephone, giving directions.

You want the person to draw exactly the figure below.

Each side of the figure is 1 inch.

Write out the directions you would give.

CHAPTER *5*

Table

You are helping design a table with a tile top.

You have 36 tiles, each 1 square foot.

How would you arrange the tiles so as many people as possible can sit around the table?

(Don't forget that they need space for plates and food.)

Draw a diagram, and explain why your plan is the best arrangement.

Midpoint Madness

The concept of midpoint is very rich in terms of its usefulness in mathematics. In each of the following quadrilaterals, find the midpoints of the sides and label them consecutively *N*, *C*, *T*, and *M*. Then draw the segments forming the polygon *NCTM*.

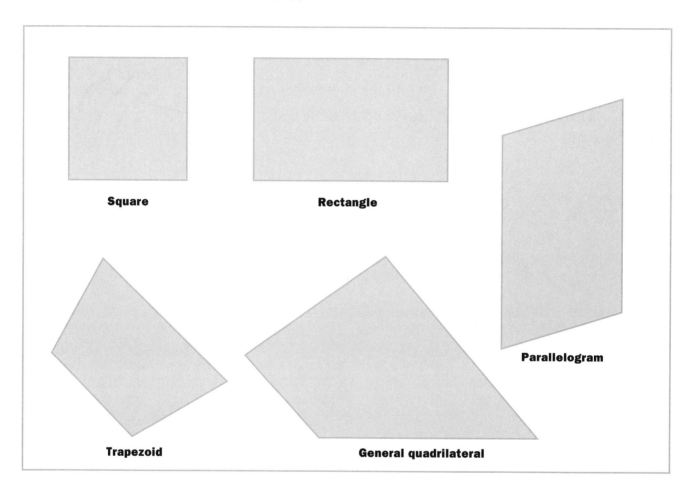

What appears to be true about all the *NCTM* polygons? _____

_____

What also appears to be true about the relationship between the area of each *NCTM* polygon and the area of its original quadrilateral? _____

_____

CHAPTER *5*

From *NCTM Student Math Notes* (1988, p. 1)

Design a Parking Lot

Date _____

This is the size of a toy car.

Work out the perimeter of the space needed to be able to park the toy car.

Record the measurements. _____

Draw the parking space around the car.

Design a parking lot in the space below.

Mark in an entrance and exit.

How many cars could be parked in the parking lot? _____

From *Gage Active Mathematics Assessment Pack, Level 2*, (Aitken 1996a, p. 86)
Reprinted with permission of Gage Educational Publishing Company, a division of Canada Publishing Corporation.

Find the Area

Find and record the area of these shapes.

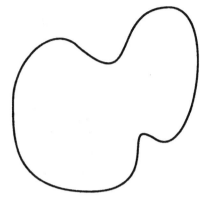

Area _____

Area _____

How did you find the area of the shapes?

CHAPTER 5

From *Gage Active Mathematics Assessment Pack, Level 2*, (Aitken 1996a, p. 23)
Reprinted with permission of Gage Educational Publishing Company, a division of Canada Publishing Corporation.

Investigating Perimeter and Area

DeCora and DeCore, interior decorators, are constructing mosaic designs using colored ceramic square tiles. Each square is the same size, and the length of a side is one unit. with six squares, they created the following designs:

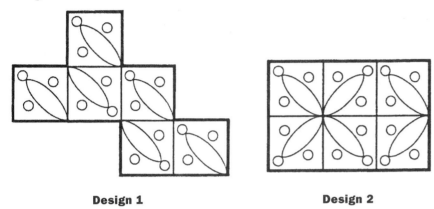

Design 1   **Design 2**

It is interesting to note that even though the areas are the same, the perimeters are different. Find the perimeter of each figure to see how they differ. To determine the price of a mosaic, DeCora nd DeCore charge $8 for each tile and $5 per unit of length for framing (1 unit of length = the length of one side of the tile).

■ Find the total cost of the tile and framing for each mosaic shown above.

Design 1 = _____   **Design 2** = _____

DeCora and DeCore often have to explain to customers that designs with the same area may have different total costs, so they need a good understanding of the relationship between the perimeter and area of polygonal figures. The following activities offer an opportunity to explore the relationship between perimeter and area using arrangements of squares. In each arrangement, neighboring squares must share a common side.

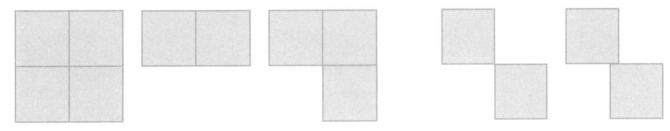

(These arrangements can be used.)   **(These cannot be used.)**

INVESTIGATING PERIMETER

You will need grid paper and fifty to one hundred square tiles or squares cut from construction paper. Let the length of the side of a square be one unit. Note that the area of each arrangement is equal to the number of squares. Work with a group of classmates to investigate the perimeter of certain arrangements made by putting squares together.

From Mumme (1988, p.1)

How Many Faces, Edges, Vertices?

Date _____

Collect six 3-dimensional solids from around the room and record their details in the chart.

Solid	Number of faces	Shapes of faces	Number of edges	Number of vertices

Write down six things you found out by looking at the grid.

_____

_____

_____

_____

_____

_____

CHAPTER 5

From *Gage Active Mathematics Assessment Pack, Level 3* (Aitken 1996b, p. 41)
Reprinted with permission of Gage Educational Publishing Company, a division of Canada Publishing Corporation.

Tessellations: Patterns in Geometry

To *tessellate a plane* means to completely cover a surface with a pattern of shapes with no gaps and no overlapping. Many designs are *geometric tessellations*.

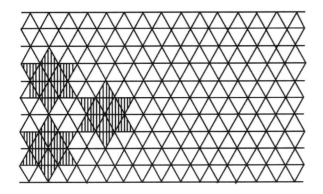

Use this triangular grid to complete the star-and-hexagon tessellation that has been started.

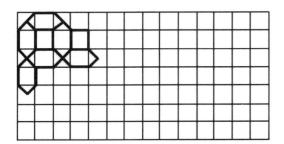

Use the lines of the square grid to help you extend the tessellation of squares and hexagons. Can you see the overlapping octagons?

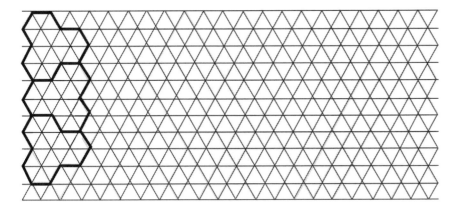

Complete a tessellation of these shapes across the page. Color your finished tessellation with three colors. Do not have two shapes of the same color touch each other.

From Seymour (1985, p. 1)

Minute Hand

Between noon on Monday and noon on Tuesday, how many times does the minute hand of a clock pass 6?

Explain how you found your answer.

Boxes of Cubes

This is a sugar cube.

It is about 1/2-inch on each edge.

There are 48 cubes in each box.

You need 1000 cubes for a school project.

How many boxes will you need?

How much space will you need to store 1000 cubes?

Look at the Graph

Date _____

What information can you find out
by looking at this graph?

Maximum daily temperature

Write six statements about things you have
found out by looking at the graph.

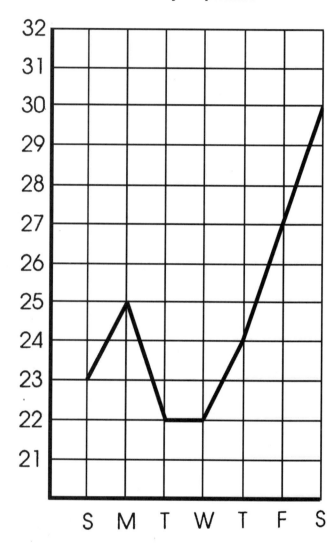

From *Gage Active Mathematics Assessment Pack, Level 2* (Aitken 1996a, p. 113)
Reprinted with permission of Gage Educational Publishing Company, a division of Canada Publishing Corporation.

How Large Is It?

A number of species of buffalo exist. The height to the shoulder and weight of several species are listed in the table.

Name (Country)	Height (cm)	Weight (kg)
Water Buffalo (Asia)	165	1000
African Buffalo	135	560
Yak (Tibet)	200	550
Gaur (Asia)	220	850
American Bison	180	1000
European Bison	200	900

Of the foregoing species of buffalo, which is the largest? The Gaur is the tallest, and the Water Buffalo and American Bison are the heaviest, but how do you determine which is the largest? A large animal is one that is both tall and heavy.

Maria has decided to add the height to the weight as a measure of the total size. The animal with the largest sum is the largest.

1. Which three animals, in order from largest to smallest, are the largest according to Maria's criterion? _____ , _____ , and _____

Jacob has decided to rank the animals from 1 to 6 for both height and weight. The smallest in each category is given a rank of 1 and the largest a rank of 6. If two animals have the same height or weight, each receives the average of the ranks they would have received. He then adds the height and weight ranks. The largest sum indicates the largest animal.

2. Which three animals, in order from largest to smallest, are largest according to Jacob's system?

_____ , _____ , and _____

Quentin has decided to find the product of height and weight as a measure of the total size.

3. What three animals, in order from largest to smallest, does Quentin think are the largest?

_____ , _____ , and _____

4. Is Quentin's method a good measure of how large the animal is? Do you think it is better or worse than Jacob's method? Explain your answer..

_____

_____

_____

From Teague (1993, p.1)

Multiply or Add?

You and a friend have two dice to play a game.

You get to go first.

You can choose whether to add or multiply the two numbers.

If you choose to multiply, you will multiply on all your turns, and your friend will add on all turns.

If you choose to add, your friend will multiply.

The winner is the first person whose dice give an answer of 12.

Would you choose to add or multiply? Explain why you chose that.

Roll Two Dice

Date _____

Roll two dice and add the numbers together. Record the total._____

Your task is to roll two dice 20 times and record the sum rolled each time.

Design a chart, table, or graph to record this information.

Write five statements about the information you have recorded on your chart.

_____

_____

_____

_____

_____

From *Gage Active Mathematics Assessment Pack, Level 3* (Aitken 1996b, p. 49)
Reprinted with permission of Gage Educational Publishing Company, a division of Canada Publishing Corporation.

Mathematical Black Holes

A *black hole*, according to astronomers, is a region in space that is so dense and has a gravity so intense that nothing, not even light, can escape. If you get near a black hole, you will always be drawn into it no matter what you do. In mathematics, a similar situation can occur. Some mathematical expressions and operations always result in a numerical "black hole" no matter where you start.

1. Follow the sequence of steps in the chart to see an example of this phenomenon. What do you notice about the final result?

_____

Steps	Try 5.	Try 7.	Try Yours.
Take any number.	5	7	
Multiply it by 6.	30		
Add 12 to the result.	42		
Divide by 3.	14		
Subtract twice the original number.	4		

Why does this procedure always give the answer 4? Let's examine the steps.

Take any number: ☐

Multiply by 6: $6 \times$ ☐

Add 12 to the result: $6 \times$ ☐ $+ 12$

Divide by 3: $\dfrac{6 \times \square + 12}{3}$, or $\dfrac{6 \times \square}{3} + \dfrac{12}{3}$,

Which simplifies to $2 \times$ ☐ $+ 4$

Subtract twice the original number: $2 \times \square + 4 - 2 \times \square$, or 4

Notice that the final result is 4, regardless of the number in the box. That is, all beginning numbers fall into the "black hole" 4.

2. Let's create a sequence of steps that leads to the "black hole" 6.

Steps	Try 5.	Try 7.	Try Yours.
Take any number.	5	7	
Multiply it by 4.			
Add 12 to the result.			
Divide by 2.			
Subtract twice the original number.			

Why does this procedure always give the answer 6? Examine the steps.

Take any number: ☐

Multiply by 4: _____

Add 12 to the result: _____

Divide by 2: _____

Subtract twice the original number: _____

3. Create a mathematical "black hole" procedure whose value is always 10.

_____

_____

4. Compare your steps with someone else's steps. Must they be the same?

_____

CHAPTER *5*

From *NCTM Student Math Notes* (1991, p. 1)

Picture Patterns

Mathematics can be visual as well as numerical. Interesting things happen when these two facets of mathematics are combined. For example, Carlos and Nancy were building a sequence based on a pattern of figures with white and shaded tiles like the ones shown.

The first three figures in their sequence are pictured.

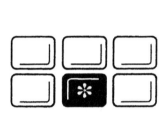

Figure 1

Figure 2

Figure 3

1. Draw figures 4 and 5 following Carlos and Nancy's "rule."

Figure 4   **Figure 5**

2. Carlos is building figure 4. How many shaded tiles will he need?_____

3. How many white tiles will Carlos need for figure 4?_____

4. How many white tiles will Nancy need to build the figure that uses 10 shaded tiles (figure 10)?_____

5. If a figure uses 100 shaded tiles, how many white tiles will it need?_____

6. How many shaded tiles will be needed for a figure that uses 21 white tiles?_____

7. How many shaded tiles will be needed for a figure that uses 22 white tiles?_____

8. How many shaded tiles will be needed for a figure that uses 15 tiles altogether?_____

9. How many shaded tiles will be needed for a figure that uses 20 tiles altogether?_____

Number Statements

Here is a set of numbers:

1, 4, 7, 10, 13, 16, 19, 22, 25, 28, 31, 34, 37

Make all the true statements you can about the set of numbers.

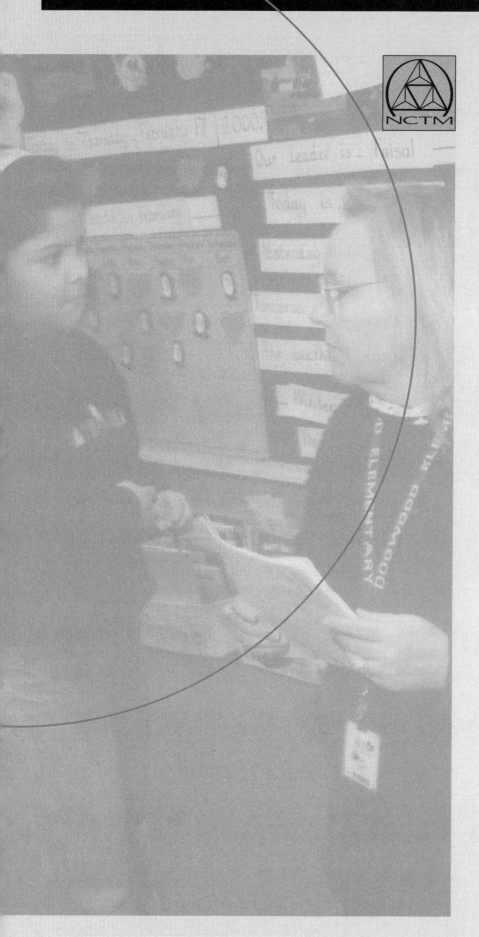

Resources

Bibliography

Aitken, E. Nola. *Gage Active Mathematics: Assessment Pack, Level 2 (3–4)*. Scarborough, Ont.: Gage Educational Publishing Co., 1996.

———. *Gage Active Mathematics: Assessment Pack, Level 3 (5–6)*. Scarborough, Ont.: Gage Educational Publishing Co., 1996.

Alberta Education. *Diagnostic Mathematics Program: Elementary*. Edmonton, Alta.: Student Evaluation Branch, 1990.

———. *Mathematics: Classroom Assessment Materials, Grade 4*. Edmonton, Alta.: Student Evaluation Branch, 1997.

———. *Mathematics: Classroom Assessment Materials, Grade 5*. Edmonton Alta.: Student Evaluation Branch, 1997.

Anderson, Judy, ed. *Constructive Assessment in Mathematics: How to Get It Going in Your District*. San Diego, Calif.: California Mathematics Council, n.d.

Archer, Jeff. "The Link to Higher Scores." *Education Week*, 1 October 1998, 1998, pp. 10–21.

Asturias, Harold. "Using Students' Portfolios to Assess Mathematical Understanding." *Mathematics Teacher* 87 (December 1994): 698–701.

Badger, Elizabeth. "More than Testing." *Arithmetic Teacher* 39 (May 1992): 7–11.

Barnett, Carne, Donna Goldenstein, and Babette Jackson. *Fractions, Decimals, Ratios, and Percents: Hard to Teach and Hard to Learn?* Portsmouth, N.H.: Heinemann, 1994.

Belcher, Terri, Grace Dávila Coates, José Franco, and Karen Mayfield-Ingram. "Assessment and Equity." In *Multicultural and Gender Equity in the Mathematics Classroom: The Gift of Diversity*, 1997 Yearbook of the National Council of Teachers of Mathematics (NCTM), edited by Janet Trentacosta, pp. 195–200. Reston, Va.: NCTM, 1997.

Billstein, Rick. "The STEM Model." *Mathematics Teaching in the Middle School* 3 (January 1998): 282–86.

Bright, George W. "Understanding Children's Reasoning." *Teaching Children Mathematics* 3 (September 1996): 18–22.

Brown-Herbst, Kari. "So Math Isn't Just Answers." *Mathematics Teaching in the Middle School* 4 (April 1999): 448–55.

Burns, Marilyn. *A Collection of Math Lessons from Grades 3 through 6*. New Rochelle, N.Y.: Cuisenaire Company of America, 1990.

Bush, William S., ed. *Mathematics Assessment: Cases and Discussion Questions for Grades 6–12*. Reston, Va.: National Council of Teachers of Mathematics, 2000.

———. *Mathematics Assessment: Cases and Discussion Questions for Grades K–5*. Reston, Va.: National Council of Teachers of Mathematics, 2001.

Bush, William S., and Anja S. Greer, eds. *Mathematics Assessment: A Practical Handbook for Grades 9–12*. Reston, Va.: National Council of Teachers of Mathematics, 1999.

Bush, William S., and Steve Leinwand, eds. *Mathematics Assessment: A Practical Handbook for Grades 6–8*. Reston, Va.: National Council of Teachers of Mathematics, 2000.

California State Department of Education. *A Sampler of Mathematics Assessment*. Sacramento, Calif.: California State Department of Education, 1994.

Chambers, Donald. "Integrating Assessment and Instruction." In *Assessment in the Mathematics Classroom*, 1993 Yearbook of the National Council of Teachers of Mathematics (NCTM), edited by Norman L. Webb, pp. 17–25. Reston, Va.: NCTM, 1993.

Chappell, Michaele F., and Denisse R. Thompson. "Modifying Our Questions to Assess Students' Thinking." *Mathematics Teaching in the Middle School* 4 (April 1999): 470–74.

Charles, Randall, Frank Lester, and Phares O'Daffer. *How to Evaluate Progress in Problem Solving*. Reston, Va.: National Council of Teachers of Mathematics, 1987.

Ciochine, John, and Grace Polivka. "The Missing Link? Writing in Mathematics Class." *Mathematics Teaching in the Middle School* 2 (March-April 1997): 316–20.

Clarke, David. *Assessment Alternatives in Mathematics*. Canberra, Australian Capital Territory: Curriculum Development Centre, 1988. (Available from the National Council of Teachers of Mathematics)

———. "Activating Assessment Alternatives in Mathematics." *Arithmetic Teacher* 39 (February 1992): 24–29.

———. *Constructive Assessment in Mathematics: Practical Steps for Classroom Teachers*. Berkeley, Calif.: Key Curriculum Press, 1997.

Cole, Karen A. "Walking Around: Getting More from Informal Assessment." *Mathematics Teaching in the Middle School* 4 (January 1999): 224–27.

Collison, Judith. "Using Performance Assessment to Determine Mathematical Dispositions." *Arithmetic Teacher* 39 (February 1992): 40–47.

Conway, Kathleen. "Assessing Open-Ended Problems." *Mathematics Teaching in the Middle School* 4 (May 1999): 510–14.

Cross, Lee, and Michael Hynes. "Assessing Mathematics Learning for Students with Learning Differences." *Arithmetic Teacher* 41 (March 1994): 371–77.

Darling-Hammond, Linda, L. Einbender, F. Frelow, and J. Ley-King. *Authentic Assessment in Practice: A Collection of Portfolios, Performance Tasks, Exhibitions, and Documentation*. New York: National Center for Restructuring Education, Schools, and Teaching, 1993.

DiPillo, Mary Lou, Robert Sovchik, and Barbara Moss. "Exploring Middle Graders' Mathematical Thinking through Journals." *Mathematics Teaching in the Middle School* 2 (March-April 1997): 308–14.

Ensign, Jacque. "Parents, Portfolios, and Personal Mathematics." *Teaching Children Mathematics* 4 (February 1998): 346–51.

Greene, Carol. *The Thirteen Days of Halloween*. Chicago: Children's Press, 1983.

Greenwood, Jonathan Jay. "On the Nature of Teaching and Assessing 'Mathematical Power' and 'Mathematical Thinking.'" *Arithmetic Teacher* 41 (November 1993): 144–52.

Helton, Sonia. "I Thik the Citanre Will Hoder Lase: Journal Keeping in the Mathematics Class." *Teaching Children Mathematics* 1 (February 1995): 336–40.

Khisty, Lena Licón. "Making Mathematics Accessible to Latino Students: Rethinking Instructional Practice." In *Multicultural and Gender Equity in the Mathematics Classroom: The Gift of Diversity*, 1997 Yearbook of the National Council of Teachers of Mathematics (NCTM), edited by Janet Trentacosta, pp. 92–101. Reston, Va.: NCTM, 1997.

Kroll, Diana L., Joanne O. Masingila, and Sue Tinsley Mau. "Grading Cooperative Problem Solving." *Mathematics Teacher* 85 (November 1992): 619–27.

Lambdin, Diana V., and Clare Forseth. "Seamless Assessment/Instruction = Good Teaching." *Teaching Children Mathematics* 2 (January 1996): 294–98.

RESOURCES

Lambdin, Diana V., and Vicki L. Walker. "Planning for Classroom Portfolio Assessment." *Arithmetic Teacher* 6 (February 1994): 318–24.

Lankford, Francis, Jr. "What Can a Teacher Learn about a Pupil's Thinking through Oral Interviews." *Arithmetic Teacher* 40 (October 1992): 106–11.

Lappan, Glenda. "President's Message: What Are Standards?" *NCTM News Bulletin* 35 (December 1998): 3.

Leitze, Annette Ricks, and Sue Tinsley Mau. "Assessing Problem-Solving Thought Processes." *Mathematics Teaching in the Middle School* 4 (February 1999): 305–11.

Lindquist, Mary Montgomery. "Assessing through Questioning." *Arithmetic Teacher* 35 (January 1988): 16–18.

Litton, Nancy. *Getting Your Math Message Out to Parents*. Sausalito, Calif.: Math Solutions Publications, 1998.

Long, Madeleine J., and Meir Ben-Hur. "Informing Learning through the Clinical Interview." *Arithmetic Teacher* 38 (February 1991): 44–46.

Maletsky, Evan. "Magic Squares." *NCTM Student Math Notes* (January 1985): 1.

Moon, Jean. "Connecting Learning and Teaching through Assessment." *Arithmetic Teacher* 41 (September 1993): 13–15.

Mumme, Judy. "Investigating Perimeter and Area." *NCTM Student Math Notes* (November 1988): 1–4.

Myren, Christina. *Posing Open-Ended Questions in the Primary Classroom*. San Diego, Calif.: Teaching Resource Center, 1995.

National Center on Education and the Economy and University of Pittsburgh. *New Standards Performance Standards*. Washington, D.C.: National Center on Education and the Economy, 1997.

National Council of Teachers of Mathematics. "Midpoint Madness." *NCTM Student Math Notes* (January 1988): 1.

———. (NCTM). *Curriculum and Evaluation Standards for School Mathematics*. Reston, Va.: NCTM, 1989.

———. "Mathematical Black Holes." *NCTM Student Math Notes*. (September 1991):1.

———. *Professional Standards for Teaching Mathematics*. Reston, Va.: NCTM, 1991.

———. *Assessment Standards for School Mathematics*. Reston, Va.: NCTM, 1995.

———. *Mathematics Education Dialogues* 1 (May-June 1998).

National Research Council, Mathematical Sciences Education Board. *Measuring Up: Prototypes for Mathematics Assessment*. Washington, D.C.: National Academy Press, 1993.

Nieding, Deborah A. "Make New Lessons, but Keep the Old: One Is Silver, the Other Is Gold." *Teaching Children Mathematics* 4 (May 1998): 514–18.

Norwood, Karen, and Glenda Carter. "Journal Writing: An Insight into Students' Understanding." *Teaching Children Mathematics* 1 (November 1994): 146–48.

Olson, Melfried, and Douglas Edge. "Picture Patterns." *NCTM Student Math Notes* (September 1992): 1-4.

Pitts, Gay. "Breathe O^2 into Your Mathematics Program—Promote Openness and Ownership." *Teaching Children Mathematics* 3 (May 1997): 496–98.

Sammons, Kay B., Beth Kobett, Joan Heiss, and Francis (Skip) Fennell. "Linking Instruction and Assessment in the Mathematics Classroom." *Arithmetic Teacher* 39 (February 1992): 11–16.

Seymour, Dale. "Tessellations: Patterns in Geometry." *NCTM Student Math Notes* (September 1985): 1–4.

Schoenfeld, Alan, Hugh Burkhardt, Phil Daro, Jim Ridgway, Judah Schwartz, and Sandra Wilcox. *Balanced Assessment for the Mathematics Curriculum: Elementary Packages 1 and 2*. Menlo Park, Calif.: Dale Seymour Publications, 1998.

Sharp, Janet, and Karen Bush Hoiberg. "The Process of Assessment Applied to Tessellations." *Teaching Children Mathematics* 4 (January 1998): 276–80.

Smith, Jacque. "Assessing Children's Reasoning: It's an Age-Old Problem." *Teaching Children Mathematics* 2 (May 1996): 524–28.

Stenmark, Jean K., ed. *Mathematics Assessment: Myths, Models, Good Questions, and Practical Suggestions*. Reston, Va.: National Council of Teachers of Mathematics, 1991.

Stenmark, Jean K., Pam Beck, and Harold Asturias. "A Room with More than One View." *Mathematics Teaching in the Middle School* 1 (April 1994): 44–49.

Stix, Andi. "Pic-Jour Math: Pictorial Journal Writing in Mathematics." *Arithmetic Teacher* 41 (January 1994): 264–69.

RESOURCES

Sullivan, Peter, and David Clarke. "Catering to All Abilities through 'Good' Questions." *Arithmetic Teacher* 39 (October 1991): 14–18.

Swan, Malcolm. "Assessing Mathematical Processes: The English Experience" *Mathematics Teaching in the Middle School* 1 (March-April 1996): 706–11.

Teague, Dan. "How Large Is It?" *NCTM Student Math Notes* (March 1993): 1–4.

Tonack, De A. "A Teacher's View on Classroom Assessment: What and How." *Mathematics Teaching in the Middle School* 2 (November-December 1996): 70–73.

WGBH Educational Foundation. *Assessment Library for Grades K–12*. Video-tapes. Boston: WGBH Educational Foundation, 1998.

Wickett, Maryann. "Investigating Probability and Patterns with *The Thirteen Days of Halloween*." *Teaching Children Mathematics* 4 (October 1997): 90-94.

Wiggins, Grant. "Honesty and Fairness: Toward Better Grading and Reporting." In *Communicating Student Learning, 1996 ASCD Yearbook*, edited by Thomas Gershey, pp. 141–71. Alexandria, Va.: Association for Supervision and Curriculum Development, 1996.

Zawojewski, Judith S. "Polishing a Data Task: Seeking Better Assessment." *Teaching Children Mathematics* 2 (February 1996): 372–78.

Zawojewski, Judith S., and Richard Lesh. "Scores and Grades: What Are the Problems? What Are the Alternatives?" *Mathematics Teaching in the Middle School* 1 (May 1996): 776–79.

Index

A

analytic rubric, 120, 121, 129

assessment types, 24–25, 89–90

Assessment Standards for School Mathematics, vii, 2, 5

C

cases, 20, 30, 41, 44, 56, 60, 71, 76, 90, 105, 118, 120, 131, 135

changing assessment practices, 4–5

checklists, 46, 48, 68–69, 93, 117, 139, 140

collections of work, 26, 52, 77–82

conferences, 42–43

criteria, 38, 118, 130

Curriculum and Evaluation Standards for School Mathematics, 2, 16, 18

E

equity, 59, 85–88

expectations, 6–7, 23

F

feedback, 70–71

G

getting started, 20

grading, 81, 118

H

holistic rubric, 120, 122, 123–124, 129

I

importance of assessment, 19

instruction
  —aligned with assessment, 18
  —decisions, 22

inventories, 47–48

interviews, 36, 42–46

J

journals, 47, 49–50

M

managing time, 91–93

multiday assignments, 24–25

N

New Standards Project, 34, 53–57, 125

O

observation, 36–41, 62–68

open-ended tasks, 28–31

open-middled tasks, 25

P

parents, 133–135

planning, 60–61, 112

portfolios, 26, 52, 77–82, 125

problem solving, 13–15, 46, 56, 69

program evaluation, 136–137

public relations, 135

Q

quizzes, 26, 51

questioning, 20, 36–37, 44

R

revising student work, 70–71

rubrics, 33, 118–125
  —definition, 118
  —types, 120–124, 129
  —examples, 119–125

S

scoring, 118–132

special needs, 85–88,

standards, 16–17, 20, 60, 85

Student Assessment Bill of Rights, viii

student self-assessment, 72–76

student work, 4–5, 6–7, 54–55, 65–67, 95–117, 126–128

T

tasks
  —developing, 32
  —evaluating, 33–35
  —expanding, 51
  —good sources, 27–29, 138–160
  —types, 8–15, 24

teacher notes, 63–68

technology, 58–59

tests, 26, 51

U

understanding, 4–5, 9, 10, 11–12

W

writing, 83–84